DYNAMITE DRILLS

FROM SUCCESSFUL COACHES AT EVERY LEVEL OF COMPETITION... THE VERY BEST DRILLS TO DEVELOP PLAYER SKILLS AND KEEP YOUR PROGRAM RUNNING IN TOP-NOTCH FASHION

Edited by Mark Dudzik and Katie Roberts

Lessiter Publications, Inc. • Brookfield, WI

Publisher's Cataloging-in Publication
(Provided by Quality Books, Inc.)

Dynamic drills / edited by Mark Dudzik and Katie
Roberts. -- 1st ed.
p. cm. -- (Winning hoops)
Includes index.
ISBN: 0-944079-35-0

1. Basketball--Training. I. Dudzik, Mark.
II. Roberts, Katie.

GV885.35.D96 2000 796.323
QBI00-500102

On the cover, University of Florida coach Billy Donovan drills a player in the finer aspects of basketball. Cover photo by NCAA Photos.
Cover and book design by Maureen Splitgerber

International Standard Book Number: 0-944079-35-0

Published by Lessiter Publications, Inc.,
P.O. Box 624, Brookfield, WI 53008-0624
For additional copies or information on other books or publications offered by *Winning Hoops* or Lessiter Publications, write to the above address.

Telephone: (800) 645-8455 (U.S. only) or (262) 782-4480.
Fax: (262) 782-1252 • E-mail: info@lesspub.com
Web site: www.winninghoops.com

Manufactured In The United States of America

FOREWORD

NO BASKETBALL COACH at any level of competition ever thinks they have enough drills in their notebooks. Everyone is constantly on the lookout for new drills to meet the changing needs of their players and teams.

That's why I think you'll find ***Dynamite Drills*** from the editors of *Winning Hoops* to be an excellent source of new drills for your program. It's packed with valuable drills used by 43 outstanding coaches at the high school and college levels. In fact, I've already marked a dozen drills that are going to be added to my own list of highly practical drills.

Featuring detailed instructions and easy-to-follow diagrams, these outstanding drills have been pulled together to meet your specific coaching needs and fine-tune your players' skills. In these six chapters, you'll find drills to strengthen the skills of your players in the critical areas of offense, ball handling, shooting, defense, rebounding, game situations, complete games, conditioning, stretching and much more.

The outstanding coaches featured in this book have shared the very best drills that have helped them more effectively prepare hundreds of players for games. Now you've got the chance to pick up plenty of new ideas that can help you do the same.

—Marty Gaughan,
Head Men's Coach,
Benet Academy,
Lisle, Ill.

KEY TO DIAGRAMS

① **Player with the ball is circled**	⁓⁓→ **Dribble**
X Defensive Player or player in line during drill	——→ **Cut**
	——┤ **Screen**
- - - -→ **Pass**	**C Coach**

NOTE:

Most of the schools listed after each coach's name are the schools each was working at when the play was originally submitted for publication in *Winning Hoops*.

Since the coaching profession is always changing, many of the coaches have since moved to new positions or relocated.

Still Want More Tips?

For hoops fans that can't get enough, you can find even more game-winning information at www.winninghoops.com.

In addition to a new play or drill every week, this *Winning Hoops* site contains quotes from notables in the world of sports and a message board that gives you a chance to sound off on hot topics in the game and correspond with coaches from around the world.

This site may put you only a few mouse clicks away from a championship!

TABLE OF CONTENTS

CHAPTER 4 — DEFENSE & REBOUNDING . . . 47-70

CHAPTER 5 — GAME SITUATIONS 71-86

CHAPTER 6 — CONDITIONING & STRETCHING. . 87-94

Chapter 1

OFFENSE

Rx For Success

REPETITIO EST MATER studiorum, which translates as "repetition is the mother of studies or learning," is an expression as old as the hills. Yet it's often forgotten in the modern classroom, where repetition and drills are viewed as tedious and boring.

Coaches must embrace this concept if they hope to be successful. Muscle memory and skill development have to be lovingly and painstakingly melded. Mastery does not come all at once, nor does it come from a coach simply telling players what to do. Players learn from hands-on experience and repetition.

There are dozens of individual moves a good offensive player needs. These are the finishing moves the good player uses after they get a step on their defender.

They are practiced every day—usually at the beginning of practice—and the whole series is timed. Since we use the game clock to control and pace our practices, the players know how much time they have to complete the series successfully.

The clock exerts its own pressure and urgency as players hustle through the exercises. There's nothing players hate more than being asked to work hard without knowing when that particular aspect of the day's practice will end.

Not knowing when the drill ends sometimes encourages players to save themselves and not put total effort into skill development—something we definitely don't want to see.

Designate the repetitions for each shot. Normally it is one, but sometimes two or three if we're returning from a long layoff or the team appears sluggish. It's much better if each player is given their own ball for the drill and rebounds their own shot. If not, use two lines of shooters and rebounders.

MOVES AT THE BASKET

1. LAYUP: Coming at a 45-degree angle to the low back, the dribbler places the ball in the box above the basket, taking full advantage of the basket's 18-inch diameter *(diagram 1).*

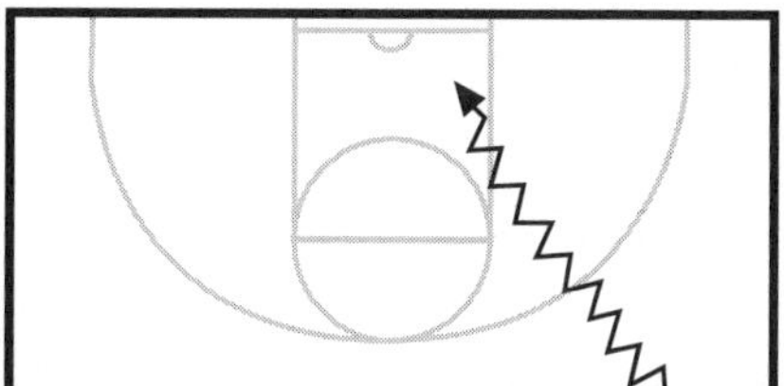

The player's palm should face the backboard on the release, as we don't want a finger roll. They should be coming off the foot opposite the shooting hand—if they are shooting right handed, their left foot is their take-off or inside foot.

For more developed players, there's the wrong foot lay-in. This involves taking a right-handed layup off the right leg. This move is valuable because your players don't always have the time nor the room for a conventional layup.

2. POWER LAYUP: Using the same line formation, stress and practice the need to develop a two-footed jump stop followed by a power move to the basket. This enables players to stay under control, withstand contact and finish with either a 1-handed or 2-handed layup. We prefer a 2-handed shot in the box.

3. REVERSE LAYUP: Players line up as described above, but drive under the basket to put up a short hook or curl shot with the opposite hand.

Discourage players from driving under the basket from the right side and using an over-the-head move with the dribble hand, in this case the right

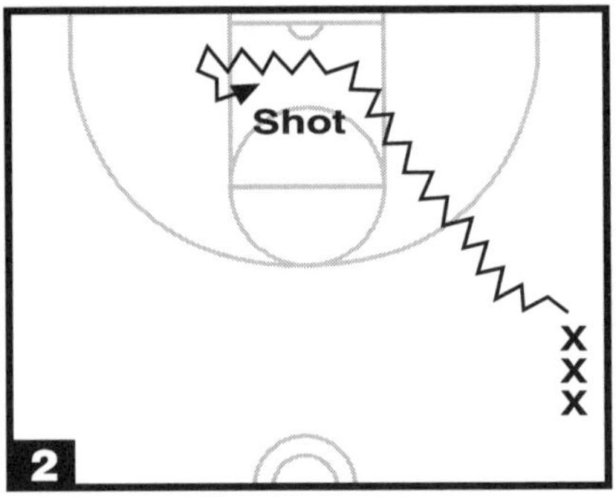

hand, because the ball is exposed and a defender can deflect it easily.

Have your players concentrate on footwork, coming off the right foot for a left-handed reverse layup or baby hook. Have them work on the use of the jump stop with the baby hook or curl shot *(diagram 2)*.

4. PULL-UP JUMP SHOT: Players drive to a spot 12 to 15 feet from the basket, come to a jump stop and go straight up, avoiding contact

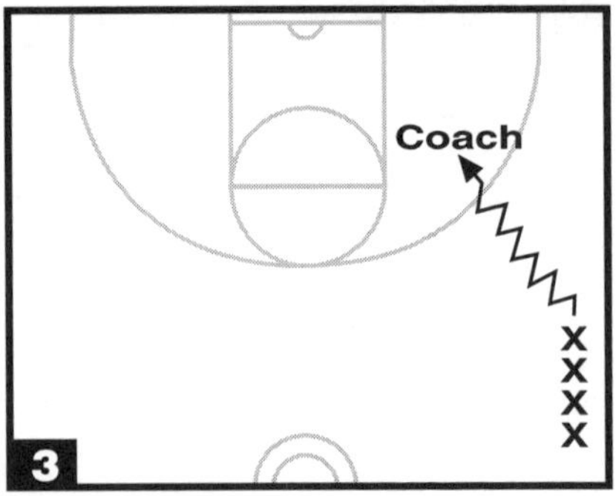

with a defender, or—in this case—the coach, and shoot the ball over an opponent's outstretched hand off the backboard.

This move keeps the player from committing a foolish foul against a defender who is positioned to take the charge. Using the backboard is critical since it softens the shot from a player who has suddenly elevated their body vertically from a horizontal drive *(diagram 3)*.

MOVES TO GET TO THE BASKET

The remaining moves combine dribble moves with jump shots and layups. If your players are unable to get to the basket to execute the moves, all is lost. The following drills combine ball handling and shooting.

5. ELBOW JUMP SHOT: Line your players up as they appear in diagram 4. Each player dribbles hard to the free-throw line extended where

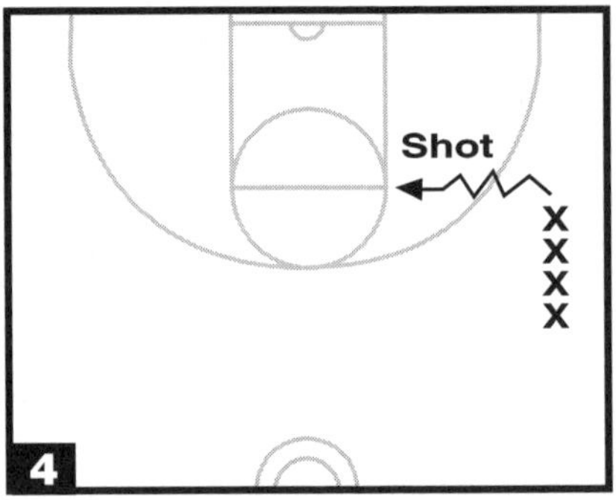

they execute one of a series of dribble moves. It may be a dribble pull back and cross over, a dribble between the legs or a dribble behind the back.

The player then heads for the elbow of the key where the free-throw line intersects the circle. Have them come to a jump stop and shoot a jump shot.

The last dribble should be a good hard bounce. After the player makes the specific dribble move emphasized each day, be sure they dribble with the outside hand—in this case the left hand. The imaginary defender will be between the dribbler and the basket sitting on the dribbler's inside hand.

6. REVERSE DRIBBLE AND LAYUP: Our philosophy allows players to use a spin or reverse pivot move on the sideline. This invites the strip or a trap because the player turns their back and cannot see an offside defender making a move. We allow this move at the elbow because there's more room to escape pressure.

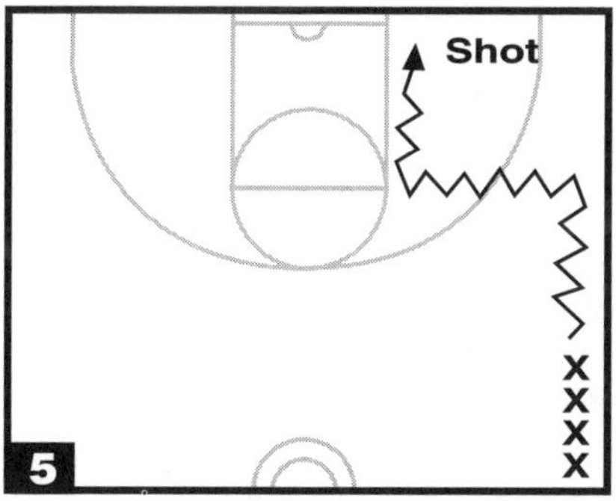

Continuing with the dribble moves listed here, the dribbler should come to the elbow, plant him or herself, reverse or spin dribble and take the ball down the line for a running hook shot off the glass. We want our players to take only 1 dribble after the spin move.

7. JUMP SHOT CORNER: Ask your players to drive the ball hard to the baseline, square up after a good jump stop and take a 12 to 15 foot jump shot along the baseline. This is not a 3-point shot. A team needs to take the ball to the baseline for a quick shot off the dribble *(see diagram 6).*

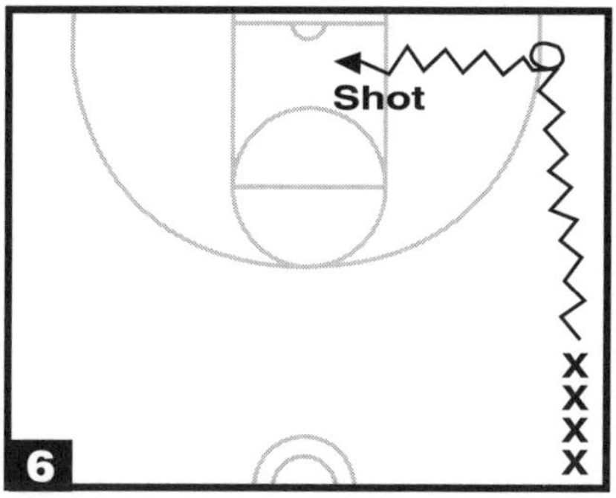

8. LAYUP OFF THE GLASS: Repeat drill 7 but instead of a jump shot, have your players use a pull-back—cross over move, a through-the-legs dribble or a behind-the-back move.

Our imaginary defender has taken away the baseline and the dribbler is unable to curl around the defender and try to go baseline. This dribble move should enable the dribbler to put the defender on their outside shoulder, providing the opening necessary to get to the basket.

We want the player to square both shoulders to the baseline as they come to a jump stop and lay the ball off the glass. Insist on the glass being used as it will eliminate the contact that comes from this move, but also because the use of the finger roll or straight-in shot without the backboard often results in a miss, negating all the work done to get to the rim.

DOWN THE MIDDLE OF THE LANE

9. RIGHT HAND LAYUP: The last series of moves begins with the dribbler driving the lane and laying the ball off the backboard. Limit the number of dribbles the player can take. Allow no more than 2 dribbles from the top of the

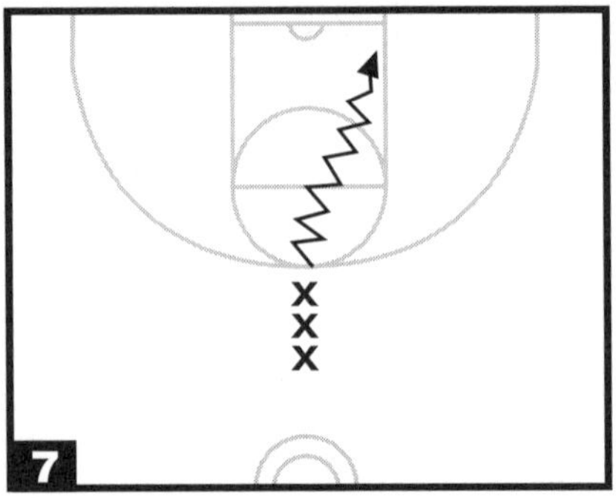

key, but only 1 dribble is permitted for the better player. This limitation ensures that players are coming quickly to the basket *(diagram 7)*.

10. LEFT-HANDED LAYUP: A good player learns to take what the defense gives them. If a defender has taken away the right side of the lane the player goes left, repeating drill #9 instead of bulling their way to the right side and into the defender.

11. LAYUP DOWN THE MIDDLE: The dribbler should drive the lane, attempting to place the ball just over the front of the rim. This is the only one of these layup drills where the backboard is not used.

12. LANE JUMP SHOT: This is the last move we work on. Players should drive hard to the free-throw line or to the dotted circle, executing a good jump stop and going up for a good jump shot. A coach should stand just below the free-throw line with their hands straight up, simulating a

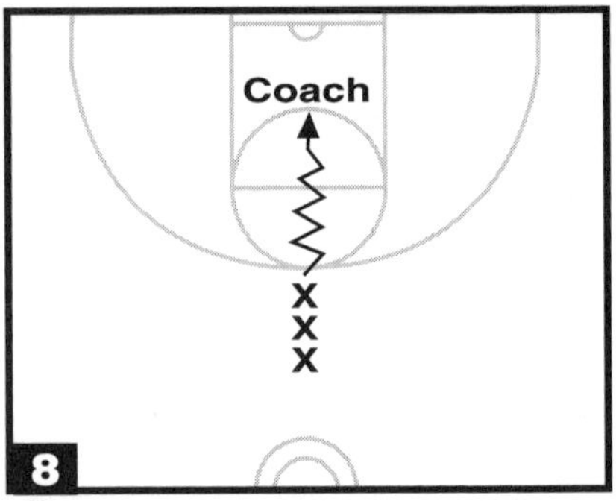

defender and forcing the dribbler to shoot over the outstretched hands of a defender *(diagram 8)*.

GREAT DAILY DRILLS

This workout will develop the skills required to finish off an offense.

After your players are familiar with what is wanted, ask them to do the same drill full court, once at each basket in a follow-the-leader style arrangement. This makes the drill one of skill development and conditioning.

The next day run the entire drill again but this time from the opposite side of the floor. By alternating back and forth from one side of the court to the other, players learn not only what they can do, but also where they need to improve.

Isn't that what coaching and teaching is all about?

–George Masters,
Fox Lane High School,
Flushing, N.Y.

Ways Of The Weave

THE WEAVE SERIES drill can be utilized with your team any time throughout the season and with its flexibility can be done with 3, 4 or upwards of 6 players.

3-MAN WEAVE

This is your typical figure-8 passing drill with 3 players on the baseline and the middle player in possession of the ball. The middle player passes to one of the sideline players and goes behind the player they threw the ball to.

The first receiver passes to the third player, cutting to the middle of the floor, and also goes behind the player. The players continue this sequence for the length of the floor. Once the ball is passed even with the free-throw line extended, the player shoots a layup.

Variations of this drill include requiring the shooter to sprint back in transition and defend 2-on-1 or coming back the other way with the passer and other offensive player.

Make each player touch the sideline after passing the ball to teach them to run wide and cover the floor with a purpose. Challenge your players to make only 4 or 5 passes to cover the full length of the floor.

Reaching the sideline may not be a reasonable guideline for younger players, but high school players are capable. If working with younger players, use cones to run around.

4-MAN WEAVE

This pattern is similar to the 3-man weave with a few differences. Have 2 defenders and 2 offensive players.

After covering the length of the floor, the team that attempted the layup immediately sets up for the front part of a press. The other 2 players must inbound the ball against defensive pressure and work it up the other end of the court for a score.

The offensive team must make 3 passes in the backcourt to eliminate the long pass and 3 passes in the frontcourt to work on offensive team fundamentals. If the defense forces a turnover, they should attempt to convert and set up the press again.

The drill ends when the offense beats the press and gets a shot attempt or secures a defensive rebound against the pressure team.

5-MAN WEAVE

This variation is an excellent drill that incorporates both offensive and defensive play. The drill starts with 5 players on the baseline and the middle player has the ball.

The player with the ball passes to the player immediately to their right or left, then goes behind both players. This sequence is followed the entire length of the court.

VARIATIONS

Have the passer and the shooter get back on defense while the other 3 players attack the opposite hoop and perform a 3-man weave.

Another step to add is to continue after the 3-on-2 with a 2-on-1 in the original direction. Similar to the other drills mentioned here, the shooter gets back and defends with the 2 defenders coming at them.

6-MAN WEAVE

This drill is the same as the others, except that you divide 6 players into 2 teams. The team whose player shot the layup immediately sets up a 3-man press and defends the other basket.

Make it a rule that the offensive team must make a set number of passes in the backcourt to avoid a long pass. If the defense creates a turnover, attempt to convert and set up the press again. If the offense breaks the press and scores, start 6 new players again.

–Mike Mondello,
University of Florida,
Gainesville, Fla.

Lightning Fast Layups

6 BASKET LAYUPS

(Involves layups, dribbling, reverse pivots and conditioning): Players line up near the basket with a ball. As the first player dribbles with their right hand to the basket and shoots a layup, player 2 follows. Each player in succession will start when the player in front of them shoots the layup.

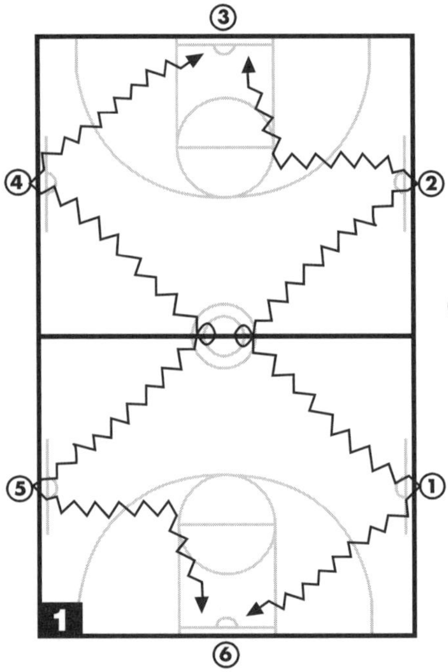

After rebounding their own shot, players dribble with the right hand to the middle circle of the main court. The player reverse pivots and heads to basket 2 for a layup. After rebounding their shot, the player dribbles toward basket 3. The procedure on the other side of the court follows with another reverse pivot in the center circle, checking for proper angle at basket 6.

We usually run 2 or 3 laps, depending on the number of players and amount of time. You can require a minimum number of makes and use pushups or laps as punishment if your players fail to make that number. Left hand layups follow a similar procedure—only use baskets in 5, 4, 3, 2, 1, 6 order with all left-hand dribbling.

LAP LAYUPS

(Involves layups, dribbling, and conditioning): Players get in pairs with one player holding a ball. The player without the ball follows the dribbler. When the first group gets halfway to the first basket, the next group begins.

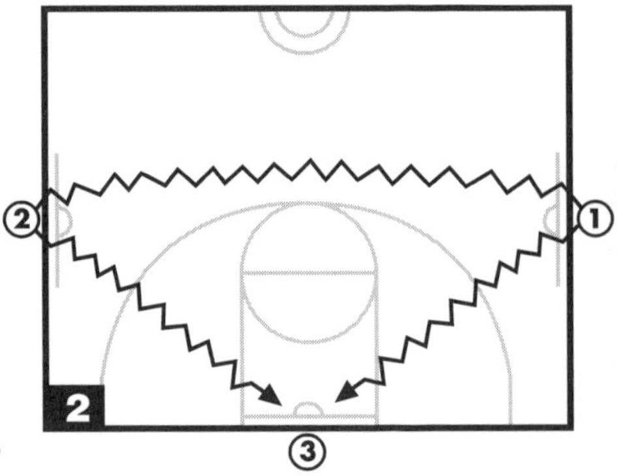

The first player dribbles to basket 2 with the right hand and shoots a layup. The partner rebounds and returns the ball to shooter, who dribbles to basket 3 and shoots a layup. The partner rebounds and returns the ball to the shooter, who dribbles to basket 1 and shoots. The partner rebounds and keeps the ball, dribbles to basket 2 where first shooter now rebounds. for left-hand layups follow a similar pattern with baskets 3, 2, and 1. Layup variations include jump stop fake and power up or reverse layups.

–Keith Siefkes,
Boys' and Girl's Varsity Coach,
Beth Eden Baptist School,
Denver, Colo.

DRILLS TO TEACH AND ENHANCE THE MOTION GAME

YOUR PLAYERS must understand both the parameters and desired results of what you want to accomplish offensively, just as with any aspect of your team's objectives.

Here are two drills that are excellent tools to teach and reinforce the building blocks of motion offense. When running these drills, it's just as important to emphasize the effective execution of fundamentals as it is to avoid turnovers due to violations.

4-BALL—THE CUTTING GAME

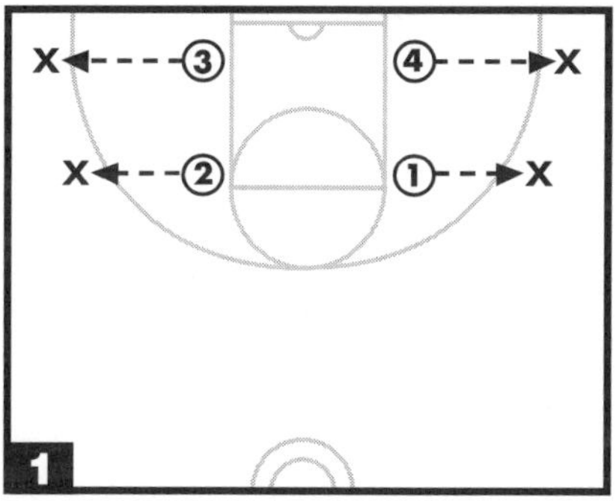

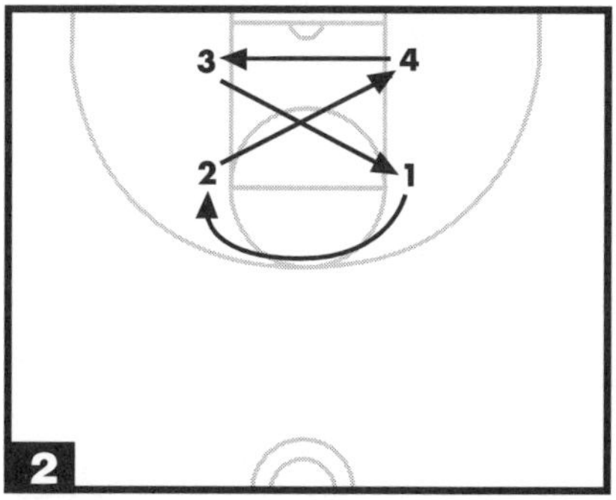

1. The inside players each have a ball.
2. Simultaneously they pass to the outside players.
Player 1 cuts and rotates to 2.
Player 2 down cuts to 4.
Player 3 up cuts to 1.
Player 4 baseline cuts to 3.

Each player needs to be at the next position as the ball is passed back from outside player.

This drill continues for 2 minutes.

MOTION AND MOVEMENT ARC

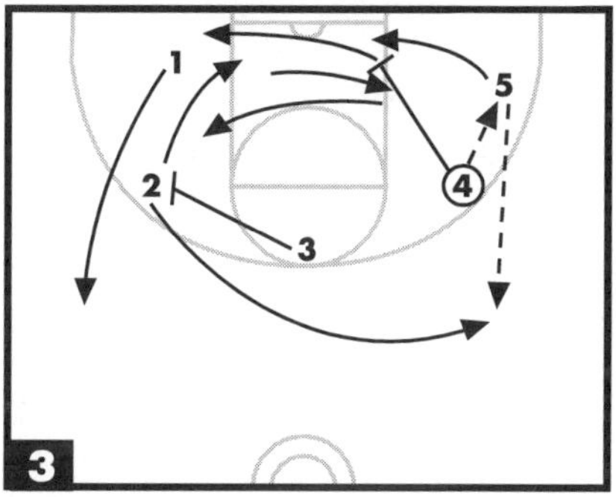

1. The ball starts with player 4 (See *diagram 3).*
2. 4 passes to 5 and cuts to the low post .
3. 3 screens for 2, who cuts to the perimeter.
4. 5 passes to 2, then cuts to the basket and screens for 4.
5. 4 passes to cutter 5 or 3.
6. 4 goes to the opposite post.
7. 2 cross-cuts to the opposite post.
8. Player 1 goes to the point.
9. Player 2 cuts high to replace 1.

–Barry Mestel,
Winning Ways,
Longwood, Fla.

Play In The Low Post

AS COACHES, you need to realize the importance of effective low post play.

One problem is finding drills that simulate game conditions in the low post. My suggestion is to take different aspects of low post play screening, such as fighting for position, outlet and catching the ball in traffic and roll them into three basic drills. These drills should improve your low players' post game.

A. CONTINUOUS SCREEN ACROSS DRILL

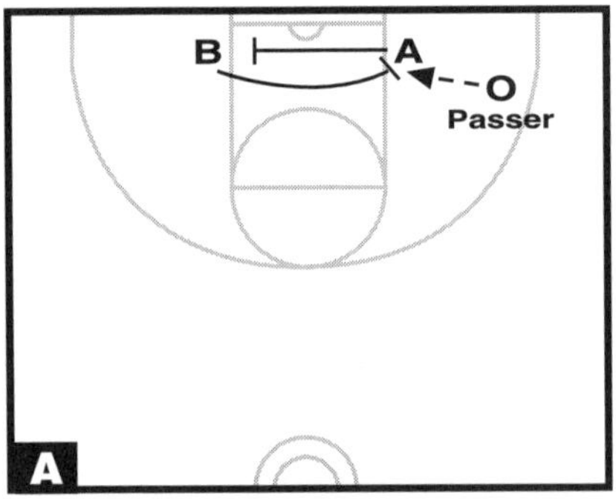

For 30 seconds, A and B screen across from one another. At any time, the passer can hit the post man for a power move.

B. 1-ON-1 IN THE POST

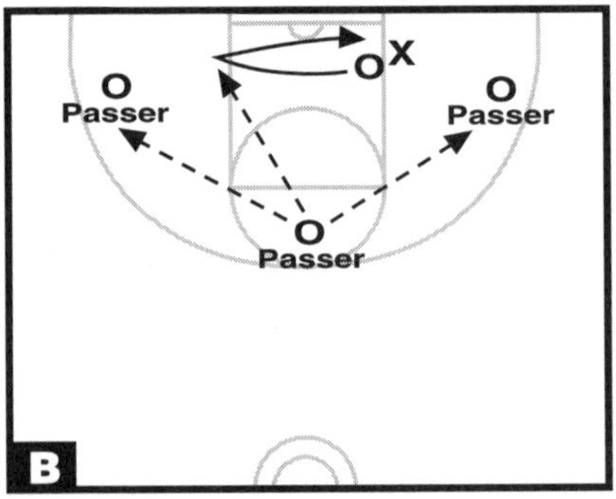

The defender plays good post defense while X battles for position. Each passer may swing the ball, with the defender following. Once the ball is tossed in the post, the passer doubles down.

C. SUPERMAN, OUTLET AND SCORE

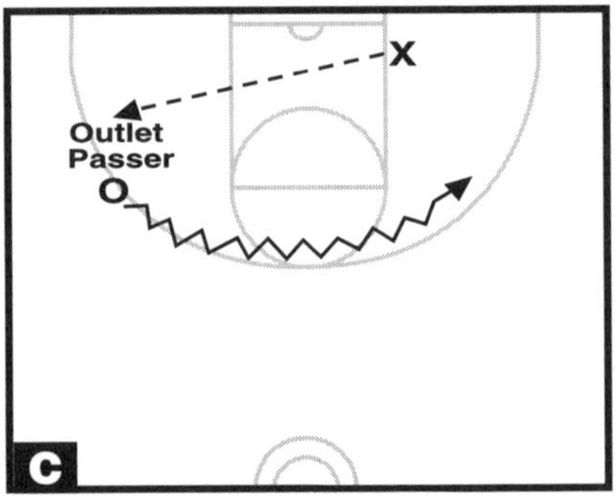

Start with a basic Superman drill by throwing the ball off the opposite board and catching outside the box. When this is done, outlet to passer then post up for move. Continue on the opposite side for 30 seconds.

–Gregory Goodwin,
Egg Harbor Township, N.J.

Hustle Layups — Right and Left-Handed Layups and Conditioning

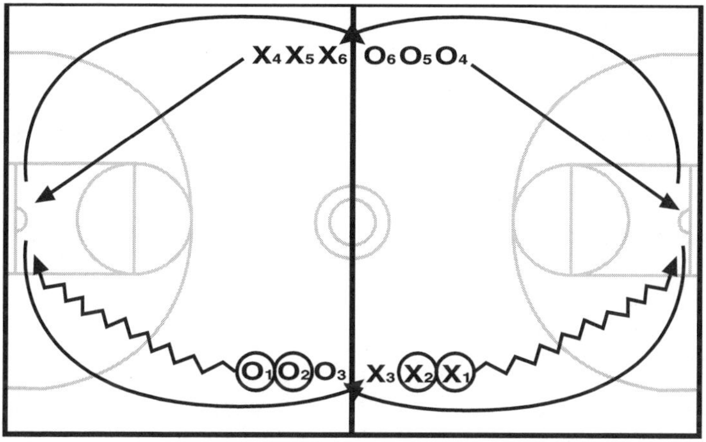

USE FOUR BALLS. Begin with X1, X2, O1 and O2. X1 and O1 dribble to their respective baskets and shoot layups, right-hand for X1 and left-hand for O1. As they shoot layups, X2 and O2 follow. As X1 and O1 dribble in, O4 and X4 run in for the rebound, making sure the ball doesn't hit the floor on the rebound.

O4 passes to X3, who dribbles in for a layup while O4 continues to the opposite end to shoot a left-handed layup after receiving a pass from X5, who has rebounded O2's layup. Pattern continues for a specified time or until a specified number of shots have been made.

Next time around, Xs and Os switch ends to get practice with both right- and left-hand layups. Note that Xs replace Xs in other line and Os replace Os. If players shoot right-handed layups, they will rebound left-handed layups and vice versa.

–Keith Siefkes,
Boys' and Girls' Varsity Coach,
Beth Eden Baptist School,
Denver, Colo.

"Everybody's got the will to win,
but few people have the will to prepare to win."
— Bobby Knight, Indiana University

Use These 20 Basketball Statistics And Theories To Your Team's Advantage

1. Missed shot attempts taken within 15 feet of the basket will bounce opposite the shooter's side 60 percent of the time, back toward the shooter 30 percent of the time and toward the middle court area only 10 percent of the time.
2. Missed balls shot from the middle court area bounce back toward the middle 80 percent of the time and to the side 20 percent of the time.
3. On free-throw attempts, defensive players having an inside position grab 67 percent of the rebounds.
4. When offensive players get the ball off a missed free-throw, they'll score 50 percent of the time.
5. Some 80 percent of all fouls are due to bad positioning.
6. Some 70 percent of fouls are committed in the offensive front court.
7. Fewer fouls are called inside the 15-foot area late in a close-scoring college game. In the same situation in a high school game, more fouls will normally be called.
8. The most common fouls occur during a blocked shot attempt, positioning for an offensive rebound, an attempt by a defensive player to draw a charge, an offensive charge or gambling for an interception.
9. The most common turnover is related to passing error.
10. The second most common turnover is due to poor footwork.
11. The third most common turnover is related to dribbling.
12. Your team's shooting percentage increases following turnovers.
13. Body balance is a factor in over 65 percent of turnovers.
14. In the late stages of a close game, the most common turnover is due to a passing error.
15. Some 67 percent of blocked shots occur within 15 feet of the basket.
16. Some 35 percent of blocked shots are due to poor shot selection.
17. Some 25 percent of blocked shot attempts lead to fouls.
18. In a jump-ball situation, the taller player's team gets the ball 65 percent of the time.
19. Players who are 6 feet 3 inches or less in height who tip the ball backward during a jump-ball situation win possession 60 percent of the time.
20. Taller players who tip the ball backward during a jump-ball situation win possession 85 percent of the time.

Chapter 2

BALL HANDLING

Dribbling Moves On The Move

PLAYER OBJECTIVES:

1. Become better dribblers.

2. Develop moves that put pressure on the defense.

3. Gain dribbling strength and quickness.

4. Become more confident.

5. Develop a repertoire for use when being closely guarded.

KEY POINT: The ball must be pounded hard and quick.

Use these words constantly during the drill, "Pound the ball, hard and quick!" Emphasize using the weak hand. You'll begin to see improvement in players within a week if this drill is done every day. Have players use their left hands one day and right hands the next.

THE DRILL

Partner players up, with one going to the end of the court facing the other. The partners must make full-court eye contact. (This is their key to go after the initial start by the coach). Have players start dribbling and running at about 3/4 speed, all the time pounding the ball hard and quick with the left hand while running directly at each other. At half court, have your players execute the drills move and continue running and dribbling. After making eye contact, players turn around and start again.

Players dribble directly at each other and execute this move on the run, brushing shoulders as they pass each other. They don't step out wide—this teaches them to read and execute moves on the run more quickly and precisely. Have players execute the move 4 to 6 times. By pounding the ball hard, players learn ball-touch control. Keep reminding them to execute the moves close and tight.

8 MOVES TO TEACH

There are 5 moves for the left hand and 5 for the right. Each move is to be executed at half court, with the players dribbling the ball hard to that point. Have them execute the move close and tight and then continue dribbling to the end of the court, where they turn around and come back at each other once eye contact is made. (Do each move 4 to 6 times.)

1. Left-hand dribble—step left, brush shoulders as players continue dribbling with the left hand.

2. Left-hand dribble—stutter step (left foot hits the floor at least four times). Have your players step left, then brush shoulders while continuing to dribble with the left hand.

3. Left-hand dribble—stutter step—then step in with the right foot. Push the ball in with the left hand. Step out with the left foot—pull the ball back out with the left hand and continue dribbling with the left hand (Call it push in, pull out).

4. Left-hand dribble—stutter step—reverse pivot. Have your players pull the ball through with the left hand, keeping it on the outside of their body and using the body to shield the ball. Push the ball out with the right hand and continue dribbling with right hand.

5. Left-hand dribble—stutter step. Cross over low and hard to the right hand, then brush left shoulders and continue dribbling with the right hand.

6. Do exactly the opposite for the right-hand dribble and you have the 10 moves on the move.

7. Jab fake and cross over 1 or 2 dribbles—jump shot—used when the defender closes out, does not react to a jab fake, takes a long drop step or gets too low while trying to stay with the player. Players pull snap the ball to their off hand, execute the reach step and dribble and pull up quickly while the defender is moving low, then shoots the jump shot. Players must jab fake and step straight ahead on the cross over move so as not to loop and give the defender an advantage.

8. Jab fake and crossover 1 or 2 dribbles—hesitation move—fake reverse and blast in for a layup. This is used when the defender closes out, does not react to player's jab fake and stays with them on the cross over move in a position that doesn't allow a jump shot.

Once a player is dribbling the ball and sees that the defender is with them, have them execute a hesitation dribble by slowing down, making a reverse fake by partially turning their body and acting as if they're going to reverse dribble. When the defender stops or slows up, they blast back in for a layup. Players must remember to jab fake and step straight ahead on the cross over move so as not to loop and give the defender the advantage.

OTHER MOVES

The following are other moves your players can work on that come once they are dribbling the ball effectively. We call them moves on the move:

Cross Over Dribble: Once players have the defender moving, have them execute a cross over dribble right to left or left to right, depending on whether they used an explode move or cross over move. Remember in the cross over dribble that the ball must be dribbled low and quick when they make the cross over to prevent the defender from making an easy steal.

Push-In—Pull-Out: This is an excellent move to get by a tough defender. Players execute the move by stepping in with the foot opposite the dribble and pushing the ball that way (right-handed dribble step to the left with the left foot and push the ball to the left with the right hand). They then step out with the other foot and pull the ball back out with the same hand (step out right with the right foot and pull the ball back out with the right hand.)

The ball is dribbled with only one hand, as it leads the defender to believe they are going to a cross over. If they're dribbling left-handed, they would step in with the right foot and push the ball to the right with the left hand, then step out with the left foot and pull the ball back out with the left hand.

When they pull the ball back out, they should blast forward quicker than they were moving. The move is designed to be executed while moving forward. The step in and step out are done while in forward motion. Have players work on this, since it's an excellent move to use.

Switch Screen: This move is used to overcome a switch by the defense on a ball screen. As players move past the screen and read the switch, they dribble once or twice. The screener opens and then crosser over or reverses and comes off another screen as the screener resets their screen. Be sure players dribble into the screen each time. It's a great move to use when the defense switches on screens because they usually are not expecting a cross over and re-screen.

–Rod Kirschner, Head Men's Coach, Horton High School, Horton, Kan.

Stay Low, Be Quick, Score

A LOT OF players have trouble staying low not only on defense, but also on offense. I created this drill for post-season workouts with perimeter players, especially the taller guards who have a tendency to dribble high and stand up.

BIG BENEFITS

Repetition of this drill will improve body position, quickness and ball handling. It creates "good habits" which will hopefully increase a perimeter player's scoring opportunities.

Use 4 cones as obstacles in this drill. Only 2 or 3 players should be at the basket. The diagrams explain the drill. It's a simple drill that when executed correctly can have an immediate impact on all players. Slower players may need to start with more distance between the cones.

The objectives of the drill are to:

- ✔ Work on ball handling.
- ✔ Maintain a low body position.
- ✔ Execute a quick change of direction.
- ✔ Create additional scoring opportunities.

Points of emphasis:

- ✦ Stay low and keep the dribble low.
- ✦ Quick change of direction, exploding to score.
- ✦ Keep eyes focused on the rim.
- ✦ Perform at game speed.
- ✦ Maintain balance when pulling into jump shot.

OPTION 1

X makes a pull back cross over move on cone 1. Attacking it right to left, the player dribbles to cone 2 with their left hand. At cone 2, they can make a low hard cross over or behind-

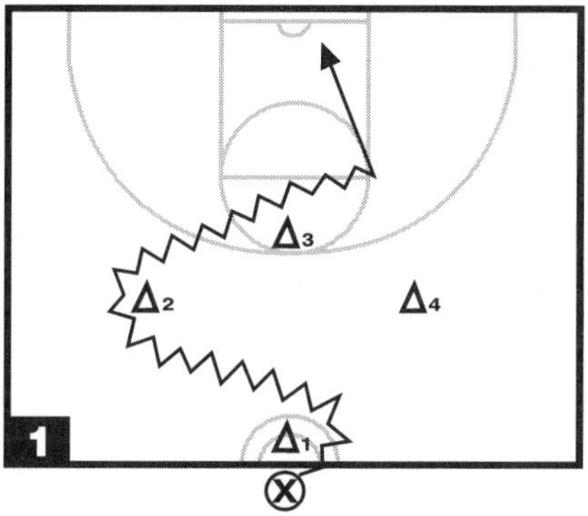

the-back dribble. With their right hand on cone 3, the player executes a hard cross over or behind-the-back and explodes with a hard dribble to score.

Have the player continue this 15 times, mixing up directions and moves.

OPTION 2

X makes a pull back cross over on cone 1. Attacking it left to right, the player then goes to cone 4 and makes a hard cross over or behind-the-back dribble past cone 4. Coming up to cone 3 with the left hand, the player makes a cross over or behind-the-back dribble and pulls up into a jump shot.

Have the player continue this drill 15 times, taking jumpers from the right and left sides.

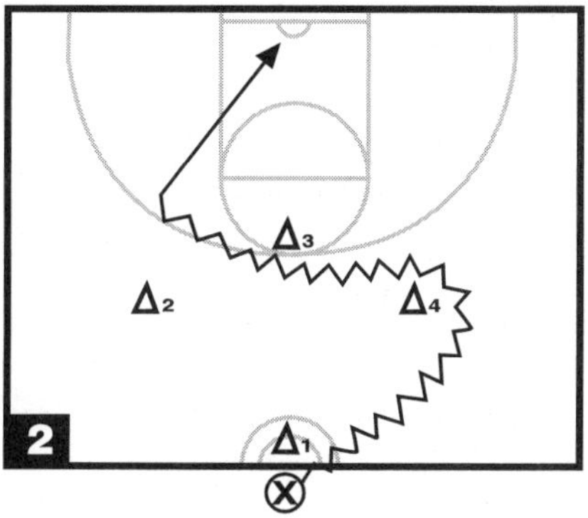

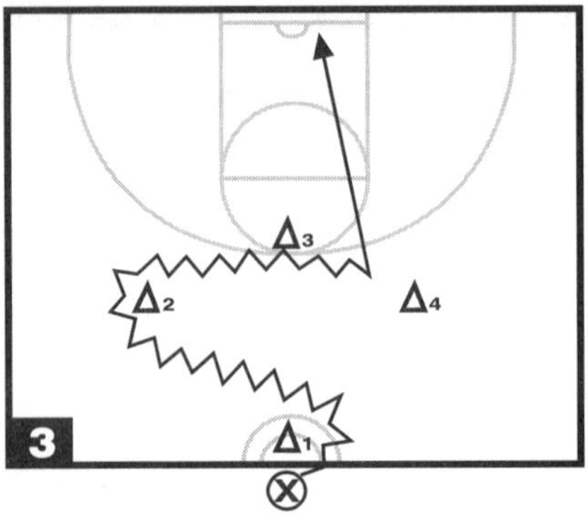

OPTION 3

Same as with option 2 but after making the offensive move past cone 2 or 4, have them pull up and shoot a 3-point field goal over cone 3. Take a total of 15 3-point field goals.

–Melissa L. Hodgdon,
Assistant Women's Coach,
Niagara University, Niagara Falls, N.Y.

KENTUCKY BALL HANDLING WORKOUT

1. *KENTUCKY 1-BALL MOVING DRILLS—NON-DOMINANT HAND EMPHASIS:* Run baseline to half court and back with non-dominant hand emphasis. Players do each move for 8 trips in "commando" fashion, then shoot 5 free throws after each set. Go hard!

a. Speed dribble—all with the non-dominant hand.

b. Hard stutter—1 time at the halfway mark each trip; all made with the non-dominant hand.

c. Cross over—Have players tart each trip with the non-dominant hand.

d. Inside out—all with the non-dominant hand.

e. Inside out/cross—start each trip with the non-dominant hand.

f. Between legs—start each trip with the non-dominant hand.

2. *KENTUCKY 2-BALL MOVING DRILL:* Run baseline to half court and back. Players make each move for 8 trips in "commando" fashion, then shoot 5 free throws after each trip.

a. Same—speed emphasis.

b. Alternate—speed emphasis.

c. Change of pace.

d. Cross them over.

3. *KENTUCKY 1-BALL MOVING DRILLS:* Players run from baseline to half court and back, going down with the right hand and back with the left hand. Each move is run for 4 trips. Player shoots free throws after each trip.

a. Hard stutter and go.

b. Cross over.

c. Inside out.

d. Between legs.

e. Combo—inside out/cross or inside out/between legs.

Total workout—100 trips plus 60 free throws. Add 10 pushups for each missed free throw of final 10 shots.

"Proper planning prevents poor performance."

Florida Gator Partner Shooting

AVE YOUR players play competitive games against their workout partner.

1. Close out shooting: Warm-up drill. Player passes the ball and closes out to their partner, then taps them in the stomach as they run by to force a higher level of concentration on the part of the shooter. Shoot 5 shots from each "Around the World" spot 2, 3, 5, 7 and 8. Shoot 5 free throws each.

2. NBA "Beat the Clock:" Player passes the ball out directly from underneath the basket and closes out, attempting to block the shot without fouling. The first shooter to hit 3 shots from the spot wins that spot.

Use "Around the World" spots 2, 3, 5, 7 and 8. Have players shoot "Sudden Victory" free throws against each other after each spot. 1 free throw each; a make beats a miss and a swish beats a make. The second shooter has the chance to tie. Keep shooting off ties until there is a winner.

3. Streak Shooter: Rebounder/passer drill. The player works the perimeter for 5 minutes. They may not shoot from the same spot twice in a row. As long as they hit, they remain as the shooter. Players stay in the same range as their partner.

On a miss, the rebounder/passer becomes the shooter and the shooter becomes the rebounder/passer. The longest consecutive streak of hits after 5 minutes wins. Follow this with 10 free throws against each other and score 2 for a swish, 0 for a make, and -1 on a miss.

4. Pitino Series: Each player passes and closes out to their partner. They then run at the ball and contest the shot without blocking or fouling. They should shoot the following sequence from the right baseline, right wing, point, left wing and left baseline. Shoot 5 jumpers from each position, then 5 shot fakes for layups, 5 shot fakes for jumpers and 5 quick dribble moves. Have players then shoot consecutively until they drain 10 free throws. The players with the least number of attempts to sink 10 is the winner.

Rob Kehoe Series "Around the World" Scoring

EACH DRILL can be done alone or with a partner as a rebounder/passer.

1. Shoot And Go: Two minutes, alternate sides. each player then goes to the free-throw line and shoots until they make 5 free throws.

2. Hit And Go: Two minutes, alternate sides. Then each player goes to the free-throw line and plays four games of "Win, lose or draw" free throws.

Players go to the line down 1 point with a bonus throw at the end of the game. Each player needs to hit their first throw to get a second. Swish= +1; make= 0; miss= -1. A miss on either shot is a loss. 2 makes are a loss. Any combination of a swish and a make is a tie. 2 swishes are a win.

3. Prove it: Three minutes, alternate sides. Player goes to the free-throw line and shoots until they swish 5 free throws.

4. Beat The Pro: Play 3 games to 12 points—HARD! also do a consecutive free-throw streak after each game. Score 1 point for a make; plus 2 for a swish and minus 2 for a miss.

STEVE ALFORD "ALL AMERICAN WORKOUT"

1. Alford Spin-Out Jumpers: 25 jumpers—spin, catch and shoot. Each player works the entire court, retrieves their shot and works on dribble moves on the way back out. Shoot 10 free throws.

2. Alford Spin Out-Shot Fake Jumpers: 25 jumpers—spin, catch, shot fake, one hard dribble and shoot. Shoot 10 free throws.

3. Alford Backboard Jumpers: Spin, catch and shoot 25 jumpers. Each player shoots from opposite sides of the lane on each shot. Shoot 10 free throws.

4. Alford Creative Jumpers: Spin, catch and create! each player should have fun attacking imaginary defenders with a variety of moves for 25 jumpers. Shoot 10 free throws.

5. Alford Attack The Chair Drill: Set the chair at the top of the key. Players start from the circle and attack straight on with a hard dribble move around the defender and into the lane. Make 10 trips. Shoot 10 free throws.

6. Alford Dribble The Lines: The player works the entire half court at full speed. Each time they come to a corner, the player changes directions. They should work on dribble, stop and go and glide with direction moves.

The player changes direction at each spot around the lane and finishes in the opposite corner from where they started. Do 2 trips starting from the right corner. Player shoots 5 free throws. Repeat from left corner. .

Total workout: 100 jumpers; 10 half court–attack the rim; four around-the-world trips of dribbling, 60 free throws.

BALL HANDLING DRILLS

PICK AND CHOOSE from these four workouts. Work for SPEED! Intense ball handling warm-ups will increase players' hand quickness, feel for the ball and strength.

BALL HANDLING: Do each move for 10 seconds hard! Players choose 1 of the workouts below before beginning their workout for the day.

WORKOUT #1: NON-DRIBBLING

(1) Slap. **(2)** Tap. **(3)** Pendulum swing. **(4)** Around the waist. **(5)** Circle right knee. **(6)** Circle left knee. **(7)** In & Out. **(8)** Pretzel flip. **(9)** See-saw flip. **(10)** Figure 8.

WORKOUT #2: STATIONARY DRIBBLING

(1) Quick cross over. **(2)** One-hand cross over with each hand. **(3)** Side push and pull with each hand. **(4)** Between legs cross each hand. **(5)** Push out each hand. **(6)** 1-2-3 cross. **(7)** Push-pull cross. **(8)** Kill each hand. **(9)** Kill cross. **(10)** Figure 8.

WORKOUT #3: TWO BALL DRIBBLING

(1) Same. **(2)** Alternate. **(3)** High low. **(4)** Fan. **(5)** In and Out. **(6)** Side push and pull. **(7)** Kill. **(8)** Cross touch. **(9)** Figure 8. **(10)** Switch 'em. **(11)** Reaction. **(12)** Doubles.

WORKOUT #4: CHALLENGES

(1) Knee-waist. **(2)** Flip roll. **(3)** Ricochet. **(4)** Ferris wheel. **(5)** Pistol Pete ricochet. **(6)** Impossible catch. **(7)** Behind the knees—drop and catch. **(8)** 2 ball windmill.

OREGON PANTHERS "PRO MOVES WORKOUT"

Half Court Scoring—"Pro Moves:" Each move is done with 3 layups and 2 pull-up jumpers from both the right and left side, for a total of 5 trips attacking the basket.

On the third layup, the player floats the ball over the "big man" in the lane. Player then attacks the press on the way back out with the same move. Have them do 5 trips from the right side, then shoot 5 free throws for each move. Have them run 5 trips from the left side and then shoot 5 free throws, then 5 trips from the center and shoot 5 free throws. Attack a chair or cone.

WORKOUT #1:

1. Magic Johnson—Pushout with 5 trips right, left, center and 5 free throws after each set (add pushout/cross and pushout/between legs/one trip each set).

2. Kevin Johnson—Between legs with 5 trips right, left, center and 5 free throws after each set.

3. Scottie Pippen—Stutter and go with 5 trips right, left, center and 5 free throws after each set.

☆ Player shoots 5 free throws at the end of the workout for a total of 45 trips, attacking in the half court and shooting 50 free throws.

WORKOUT #2:

1. Jason Williams—Bounce back, cross over with 5 trips right, left, center and 5 free throws after each set.

2. Penny Hardaway—Killer cross over with a between legs/crossover—five trips right, left, center and 5 free throws after each set.

3. Kenny Anderson—Between legs/behind back with 5 trips right, left, center and 5 free throws after each set.

☆ Each player shoots 5 free throws at the end of the workout for a total of 45 trips, attacking in the half court and shooting 50 free throws.

WORKOUT #3:

1. Earl the Pearl—Spin with 5 trips right, left, center and 5 free throws after each set.

2. Penny Hardaway—Half spin, hesitate and go with 5 trips, right, left, center and 5 free throws after each set.

3. Michael Jordan—Player slows into a hesitation move, explodes into a crossover through the lane for a layup, a pushout for a layup, or pull back cross over into a jumper. 5 trips right, left and center with 5 free throws after each set.

☆ Player shoots 5 more free throws at the end of the workout for a total of 45 trips attacking in the half court and shooting 50 free throws.

"Hard work will not guarantee you anything, but without it you don't stand a chance!"
— Pat Riley, Miami Heat

REGGIE MILLER'S "SHOOTING OFF THE DRIBBLE" WORKOUT

EACH PLAYER STARTS with a spin out and catch on the perimeter anywhere from 15 feet to 3 or 4 feet outside the arc, using the whole court. The Players should use a variety of set ups—catch and rip, jab, catch and lift, shot fake.

The player needs to be a quick decision maker as if in a game situation. In a game they would shoot off the catch, make a quick move, or pass the basketball.

1. Shoot off the spin and catch 25 shots.

2. 1 dribble with the right hand and then shoot. 25 shots.

3. 2 dribbles with the right hand and shoot. 25 shots.

4. 1 dribble with the left hand and shoot. 25 shots.

5. 2 dribbles with the left hand and shoot. 25 shots.

6. 3-dribble sequence into the shot off the dribble.

A. Cross over (right—cross dribble with left—another left; alternate with left—cross dribble with right—another right). 25 shots.

B. Inside out (right—inside out—another right; alternate with left—inside out—another left). 25 shots.

C. Between the legs (right—through—left: alternate with left—through right). 25 shots.

D. Change of pace or step back move—vary the timing. 25 shots.

- Player shoots 100 free throws after each set of 25 shots.
- Total workout—225 shots plus 80 free throws.

"It's not necessarily the amount of time you spend at practice that counts. Instead, it's what you put into the practice."
— Eric Lindros

3-POINT BLITZ!

PARTNER SHOOTING WORKOUT

- ✗ All 3-point shots.
- ✗ Shooter works with rebounder/ passer off the pass and catch.
- ✗ Player shoots 5 free throws after each set of 3s.
- ✗ Player alternates with partner.

WORKOUT #1

1. Shoot 20 3pointers from the #2 spot. 5 free throws.

2. Shoot 20 3 pointers from the #3 spot. 5 free throws.

3. Shoot 20 3 pointers from the #4 spot. 5 free throws.

4. Shoot 20 3 pointers from the #6 spot. 5 free throws.

5. Shoot 20 3 pointers from the #7 spot. 5 free throws.

6. Shoot 20 3 pointers from the #8 spot. 5 free throws.

7. Shoot 20 3 pointers from the #5 spot, counting attempts. Have your players shoot free throws until they swish 10.

Total workout: Approximately 150 to 160 3 pointers plus 40 to 50 free throws. Estimated workout time for this drill is 40 to 45 minutes.

WORKOUT #2

- ✗ Each player shoots 10 3 pointers at each spot instead of 20 for a quicker version of workout #1. Estimated time is 20 to 25 minutes.

WORKOUT #3

1. Have each of your players shoot the following shots in succession, starting from the #2 spot and catching all passes outside the 3-point line:

- ✓ 5 3-point shots.
- ✓ 1 shot taking one dribble right (2- or 3 point shot).
- ✓ 1 shot taking one dribble left (2- or 3 point shot).
- ✓ 1 shot using a shot fake and 1 dribble right (3-point shot).
- ✓ 1 shot using a shot fake and 1 dribble left (3-point shot).
- ✓ 1 shot with a step back moving right (3-point shot).
- ✓ 1 shot with a step moving left (3-point shot).
- ✓ Layup.
- ✓ Shoot 3 free throws.

2. Repeat from the 3, 4, 5, 6, 7 and 8 spots. Total: 35 threes, 40 twos, 7 layups and 21 free throws.

"The mind is the limit.
As long as the mind can envision the fact,
the satisfaction is knowing that you did your best
to become the best you are capable of becoming."
—John Wooden, Former UCLA Men's Coach

Advanced Finishing Workouts "NBA Finishing" 3 Ways to Finish

HAVE YOUR PLAYERS do both of these to finish 6 times from the right side and 6 times from the left side. Player goes 3 times to the baseline side and 3 times to the middle.

1. KOBE BRYANT "REVERSE LAYUP"

Use the same attacking sequence but this time when player is about to enter the lane, have them take one more dribble to get deep, then reverse and finish on the opposite side of the basket. As they increase their ability to explode and "hang," have them go "up and under," starting on one side of the basket and finishing on the other.

Have them make 3 trips to the baseline side from each side followed by 5 free throws. Players make 3 more trips attacking the middle followed by 5 free throws. This gives your players 12 trips from each side plus 10 free throws.

2. PENNY HARDAWAY "TWIST AND SCORE"

Once player is deep in the lane have them come to a 2-foot jump stop. They then shot fake and use both a step in and score and a step through and score. Have your players make 3 baseline trips from each side, followed by 5 free throws. Make 3 trips into the middle followed by 5 free throws for a total of 12 trips from each side plus 10 free throws.

3. JASON WILLIAMS "HIGH OFF THE GLASS"

Place a chair just inside the arc. Have the player rip the ball low and attack the basket. As they start their layup, the player should imagine a tall defender coming down to disrupt the shot.

The player lays the ball high and soft to the corner of the square and drops it through the hoop. When attacking the middle area, have them arc the ball soft over the front of the rim and over the defender.

Have your players alternate sides. After attacking from the right side, the player retrieves the ball and attacks the press through the chair on the opposite side on the way back out.

Each player shoots 5 free throws after 3 trips attacking the baseline from each side. They then attack the middle for 3 more trips from each side, then shoot 5 more free throws. This gives them a total of 12 trips from each side, plus 10 free throws.

"The country is full of good coaches. What it takes to win is a bunch of interested players."
— Don Coryell

"SHOOT-A-WAY"

THIS TOTAL WORKOUT will include 48 trips finishing in the lane and 40 free throws.

WORKOUT #1

3-POINT SHOOTING WORKOUT, SPOT UP EMPHASIS, 350 "3S" PLUS 50 FREE THROWS.

Drill #1. "Steve Kerr's Spot Ups." 9 spots with 11 shots at each spot: baseline; first lane spot; wing; elbow; straight up; same on opposite side. Each player shoots 12 shots at the top of the key for an even 100 shots, including 10 free throws after the first 5 spots are done. Do free throws after all 9 spots are done. 100 shots.

Drill #2. "Dan Majerle's Heat." 7 spots: baseline, wing, elbow, straight up, elbow, wing, and baseline. Each player makes 5 shots before moving to the next spot, keeping track of their personal record for least attempts to make 35 shots. Shoot 10 free throws. Approximately 60 to 70 shots.

Drill #3. "Larry Bird's NBA Downtowns." 5 spots with 10 shots from each spot: baseline, wing, straight up, wing, on baseline. Player spots up 2 to 3 feet behind the arc. 10 free throws. 50 shots.

Drill #4. "Jason Williams Machine Gun." 5 spots. This is a drill for great shot preparation with feet set, body down, hands ready. Catch and step into the 3-point shot and stay at each spot for 1 minute. The passer should deliver the next pass as the shooter resets and locates the passer after previous shot .

Player should get a high volume of shots in a short period of time without compromising either form or execution. The goal is to quicken the release of the shot with accuracy. Players should shoot 10 free throws after the first 4 spots are complete. Shoot 10 more after the last set of 1 minute. Approximately 150 shots.

WORKOUT #2

3-POINT SHOOTING WORKOUT, SHOOTING ON THE MOVE EMPHASIS, 240 "3S" PLUS 60 FREE THROWS.

Drill #1. Steve Alford Rapid Fire." Player moves from baseline to wing in "rapid fire" fashion and shoots 10 shots from each spot for a total of 20 shots. Now they work wing to elbow for 10 shots each spot, for a total of 20 more shots. Advance to elbow-to-elbow for 10 shots each, or 20 more.

Shoot 10 free throws. The player finishes on the other side, first working elbow, wing for 20 total, then wing, baseline for the final 20. Shoot 10 more free throws. Total of 100 shots.

Drill #2. Michael Jordan's Dribble Treys." 7 spots with 10 shots from each spot: baseline, wing, elbow, straight up, elbow, wing, baseline. Add a chair. Lift, jab, shot fake, etc., and attack with a 1-dribble move into their jumper.

Player dribbles back with the opposite hand with a one-dribble move into their jumper. Take 5 shots on each side of the chair at each spot for a total of 10. Shoot 10 free throws after the first 4 spots and 10 more once drill is completed for total of 70 shots.

Drill #3. Reggie Miller's NBA Bombs. 7 spots with 10 shots from each spot: same spots as #2. Again add a chair.

Player comes straight out as if off a

downscreen or straight cut action and hits a 3-pointer; fade back to the other side of the chair for the other 3-pointer. Take 5 shots on each side of the chair at each spot for a total of 10 at each spot. Shoot 10 free throws after the first 4 spots and 10 more once complete for a total of 70 shots.

WORKOUT #3

3-POINT SHOOTING WORKOUT, TRANSITION EMPHASIS, 260, "3S" PLUS 70 FREE THROWS

Drill #1. "Steve Kerr/Larry Bird Combination 3s." 7 spots. each player spots up and shoots 5 shots at "inside" 3-point range, then backs up and shoots 5 NBA "outside" 3-point range for 70 shots. Have your players finish by shooting 10 free throws.

Drill #2. "Kobe Bryant Transition 3s." The player takes the ball on the dribble from half court and pulls up off the dribble for the 3-point shot. Make sure they are clearly behind the arc to shoot 10 from the right side, 10 from the left side and 10 from the center. Finish by shooting 10 free throws.

Each player goes back and attacks off the dribble from half court, this time making 1 hard dribble move into the 3-point shot, stutter and step back, cross over, inside-out, etc. Shoot 10 from the right side, 10 from the left side and then 10 from the center. Shoot 10 free throws for a total of 60 shots.

Drill #3. "Allen Iverson Run And Gun 3s." The player runs from half court up the right sideline and catches the ball outside the arc, near the free-throw line extended. Spot up and shoot the 3-pointer. The passer should throw the 1-2 pass and the 3-4 pass for the proper transition "3" angle.

Each player takes 15 shots from the right side, 15 from the left side and then 10 free throws. Repeat each side for 10 more shots, this time making a shot fake and taking 1 clear dribble, working both directions to the baseline or back toward the top. Shoot 10 more free throws for a total of 60 shots.

Drill #4. "Glen Rice Catch, Turn And Shoot!" The player starts in the block area for all 6 spots and runs out to the right baseline as if coming off a down screen and shoots the 3-pointer. Concentrate on having your players turn into the ball as they come off the screen. Have them come out to the corner for 10 shots, to the wing for 10 shots, to the elbow for 10 shots and straight up for 10 shots.

Shoot 10 free throws. Repeat on the opposite side for the final 3 spots. Shoot 10 more free throws. 70 shots.

***Note**—2, 3 and 4 can work with just a player and your partner or up to 4 to 5 shooters and 1 passer. Have players retrieve their own ball off the rack and send it to the passer. They could also work a rotation consisting of shoot, pass and retrieve.

The drills on pages 19 to 28 were gathered and modified from various high school, college and professional programs and are used successfully by Kevin Bavery, Head Men's Coach at Oregon Senior High School in Oregon, Wis.

Drills To Perfect The Dribble

PURPOSE: Develop individual offensive skills while focusing on the ability to score while utilizing the dribble.

ORGANIZATION: *(diagram 1).* The dribble series can be effective with any number of players using full or half court. The optimum number for full court would be 11 to 13 players, with 3 to 6 for a half court drill.

1. Each player has a basketball.

2. Use single-file lines at half court.

3. Position a player, manager, cone or chair near the 3-point line as a defender.

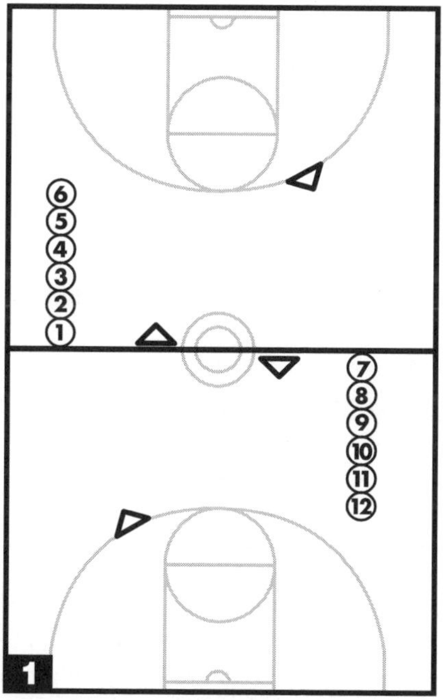

DIAGRAM 1: Organization: This is the setup for the right-hand dribble series. Each player has a ball in single-file lines at half court. This example shows the utilization of the full court. Cones are placed at the 3-point line to serve as defenders. Place cones at half court to indicate where each player dribbles to after rebounding their own shot.

TEACHING POINT

1. Start players at half court.

2. Have the player execute a full-speed dribble with their outside hand (a variation would be to use the inside hand).

3. Have the player execute the designated offensive move close to the manager or cone. We emphasize going "body to body" past the defender.

4. Utilize hard dribbles with the head up (eyes on the rim) and good balance.

5. Player finishes with a layup or dunk. (We also do the dribble series, shooting jump shots instead of layups).

6. After shooting, the player dribbles full speed to half court on the opposite side of the court *(diagram 2).* Each player then goes to the back of the line.

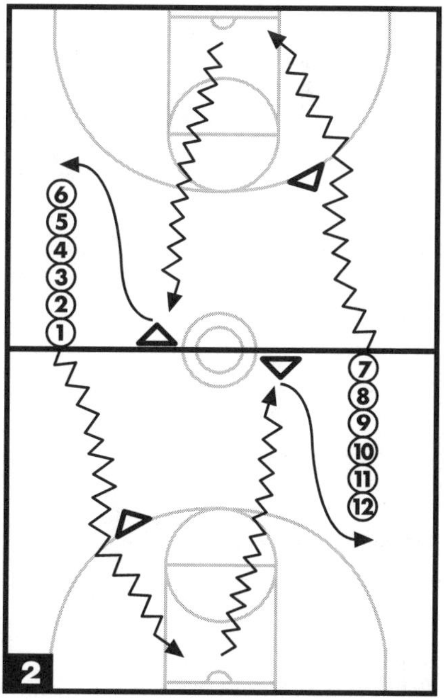

DIAGRAM 2: Teaching Points: Player #1 dribbles hard at the cone, executes the designated move and finishes the play with a strong layup or dunk. Player #1 gets their own rebound and dribbles full speed to the cone at half court. Player #1 then gets in line behind player #12. Player #7 is executing the same sequence as player #1 at the other end of the court. Complete each move once on each end of the court.

DRIBBLE SERIES PROGRESSION

1. Hesitation/stutter.
2. Behind the back.
3. Between the legs.
4. Cross over.
5. Double cross over.
6. In and out.
7. Behind the back and between the legs.
8. Between the legs and spin move.
9. Cross over and behind the back.

There are many possibilities for various combination moves.

VARIATIONS

1. Right-hand dribble, shoot layups.
2. Left-hand dribble, shoot layups.
3. Right-hand dribble, shoot jump shots.
4. Left-hand dribble, shoot jump shots.
5. Add possible transition shots:
   - Baby jumpers.
   - Free-throw line jump shot.
   - Any of the dribble series moves from the top of the key or free-throw line.
6. When shooting layups, have players finish some of the moves with a 2-foot jump stop or a power layup. You can also add a shot fake.

CONCLUSION

The dribble series provides an opportunity for each player to improve their offensive skills. Emphasis must be given to using maximum effort and correct technique at all times.

–Chuck Carringer,
Head Boys' Basketball Coach,
Oak Ridge High School,
Oak Ridge, Tenn.

North Carolina State Ball Handling Workouts

1. TIGHT CHAIRS:

Place 4 chairs or cones about 3 feet apart in a straight line. Have players execute the following dribbling moves while going through the chairs. Each move is done by going down through the chairs and back.

The emphasis of this drill is to help your players become more ball quick. Make sure they're going right at the chair as often as possible.

WORK ON THE FOLLOWING MOVES:

A. Cross over.

B. Inside out right hand.

C. Inside out left hand.

D. Inside out and cross over.

E. Between the legs.

2. SPREAD CHAIRS

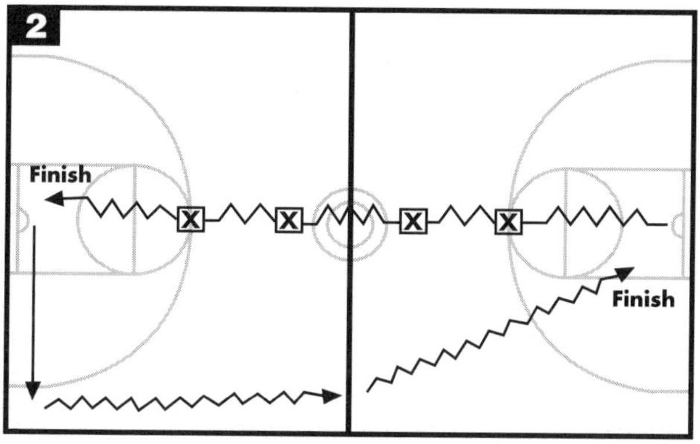

Place one chair at the top of the key, another toward half court on the circle, one chair on the other half court on the circle and the last chair at the top of the key on the opposite end.

The emphasis of this drill is for players to get the ball out in front of them and really go hard. Begin the drill with players starting on the baseline with the ball. The player goes hard at the first chair and executes their first dribble move.

Each time a player gets to a chair they execute the dribble move, going hard past the last chair and finishing. Always vary the way they finish. Sometimes you may want the players to shoot the pull-up jumper, while other times you may want them to shoot a reverse layup. Other ways to finish include high off the glass, Stockton or shoot the runner.

Upon finishing, the player takes the ball out of the net and gets wide on the baseline. They then take the ball hard to half court (using as few dribbles as possible) and execute the same dribble move they made against the chairs. The player takes the ball hard to the basket and finishes.

They'll make one trip using each of the following moves:

A. Hard stutter left hand.
B. Hard stutter left hand.
C. Cross over (executed twice).
D. Inside out right hand.
E. Inside out left hand.
F. Inside out and cross over.
G. Between the legs.

3. HALF COURT DRIVES

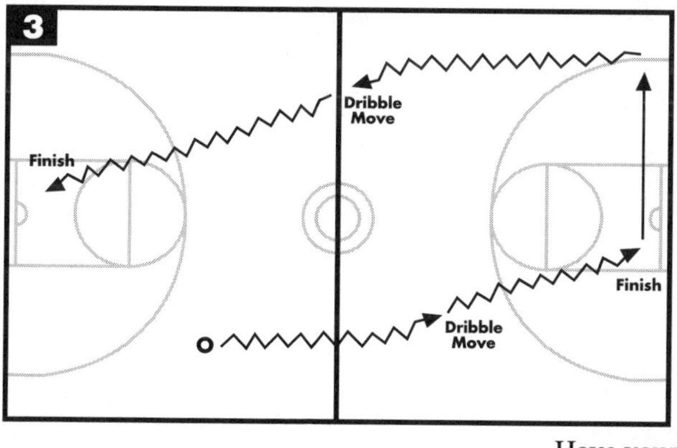

Start the drill at 3/4 three-quarter court and vary where players make their dribble move. Each player starts with their back to the basket and see-saws the ball behind their back. Once they're on the right side, they'll turn and go hard with their right hand.

Have your players vary their finishes and the point where they'll make the dribble move. After scoring, have the player get wide on the baseline, square up and go hard to half court.

The player then executes a dribble move on the way back to half court and should remember to break the tape at half court (they should break the line at half court as a sprinter would at the finish line).

HAVE YOUR PLAYERS WORK ON THE FOLLOWING MOVES:

A. Blast.

B. Hard stutter right hand.

C. Cross over.

D. Inside out.

E. Inside out and cross over.

F. Between the legs. After the player shoots 5 free throws, they repeat this sequence on the left side of the floor.

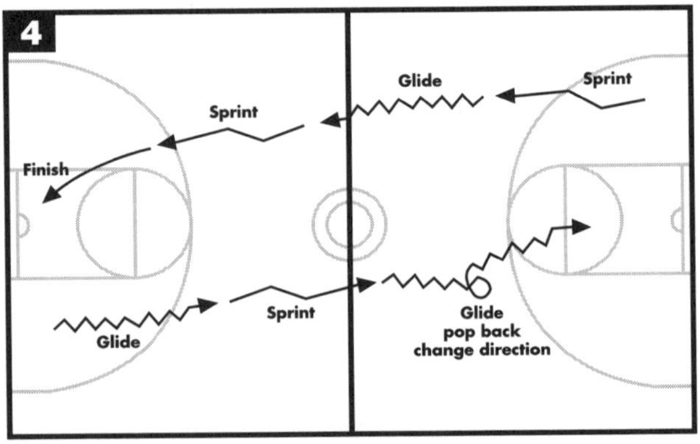

4. 4 FULL-COURT TRIPS OF GLIDE DRIBBLE

The player starts with a blast dribble and then gets into their glide. Simulate the defender getting on their shoulder and then create space by bouncing back and exploding forward or by going foot-over-foot (blasting by them). Players vary finishes at the end of each trip.

5. 3 SETS OF COMMANDO

We've changed this drill. Instead of working from the baseline to the free-throw line, we're now working from the baseline to the half-court line. This is more specific to playing the game and does a better job of simulating blasting by the defender.

6. 2 SETS OF KILL THE GRASS

Have your players stay in a circle and work on being ball quick.

7. END THE WORKOUT WITH 6 BASKETS IN 30 SECONDS

Players must make 6 full-court layups in 30 seconds.

Keep the following points in mind during the workout for each player:

1. Shoot 5 free throws to rest after each drill segment. Have players record them in their workout book.

2. This should be an intense 25 to 30 minute workout.

3. We are constantly working on the same moves during this workout but vary the way we work on them.

4. Vary the way players finish. Don't allow them to finish with the same type of shot every time.

–Eddie Andrist,
Head Men's Coach,
University of Wisconsin—Stout,
Menomonie, Wis.

Chapter 3

SHOOTING

ART OF SHOOTING DRILLS

WHEN LEARNING to shoot and improving shooting, it's important for players to learn how to check their own shot. For this reason, we have built our shooting style around four checkpoints during which players check themselves before, during and after the shot.

By using these and the hand and foot techniques we mention—along with constant repetition and practice—you will develop better shooters. With a little coordination, a lot of hard work and hours of practice, they can become outstanding shooters.

Outstanding shooters are made through repetition and proper practice—they are not born.

FOOTWORK IS CRITICAL

Footwork is important to good shooting. Except for free throws where the feet are parallel, your players should have the foot of the shooting hand slightly forward. The feet should be about shoulder width apart with the back foot toe even with the front foot arch. Both feet should be facing the basket, as this will give them maximum strength when they release the ball.

Have them always bend their knees when shooting and as the ball passes in front of the eyes, extend the knees as if they were pushing the toes through the floor. Be certain the front foot stays in front, even when they come down on the jump shot. Don't let them curl their legs up when they shoot–keep them straight. All shooting strength is done by the legs—the hands and arms serve only as guides.

HAND POSITION

Hand position is the next in importance. The player's index finger should go on the middle of the ball, across the seams. On most balls, the insignia, name and valve core are centered with the seams. Their thumb and little finger should be even on the ball or from the seam. This will keep the elbow in.

If your players are having a problem with this, check the thumb and little finger to be sure they're even. The guide hand should be on the side of the ball, forming a "T" with the thumb or the shooting hand. It should only guide the ball into the shot pocket—the thumb and palm should not turn as the ball is shot. Players should face the forearm as if to grasp it.

The ball should be resting on the upper parts of the fingers—not on the pads of the knuckles or palm. This will give players a good soft shot and allow them to control their shot while using their shooting strength as it comes from the legs. There should be a visible space between the knuckles and the ball.

WHERE ARE THE HANDS?

Be sure to check the player's hand placement on the ball, with the fingers pointing upward and wrinkles in the wrist. This position gives players the all-important "wrist cock."

The shooting arm should form a "U" with the hand, forearm and upper arm. The thumb of the shooting hand should form a "T." This position should not change; rotation of the ball to the shot pocket should be from the shoulder.

The ball should be kept close to the body on the shooting hand side, as the shoulder rotation will allow players to keep the ball protected. It is very important to keep the wrinkles in the wrist, the wrist cocked and rotate from the shoulder. Most of this will take place while a player is in the shooting position or triple-threat position.

SHOT POCKET POSITIONING

The second checkpoint is bringing the ball up and into the shot pocket. The arm should rotate at the shoulder—not the elbow—until the elbow is under the ball and the player can see the basket under the ball and between both arms (the shooting window).

The wrist is now back, palm up with fingers pointing toward the head, forming a "C" with the ball resting on the upper parts of the fingers. Taking the guide hand away, the ball should stay on the hand without falling off. The index finger, wrist, elbow, shoulder, hip, knee and toe should be in a straight line facing the basket.

As the ball was brought up, the index finger should have passed directly in front of the eye on the same side as the shooting hand. Have your players concentrate on a target, looking directly at a spot at the front of the rim.

Using the net rungs as the target, they will notice that most rungs have the shape of a "W." Have them keep their eyes on the "W" through the entire shot, never taking them off it.

As the ball passes in front of the eyes, they should explode with their legs either onto the toes or jumping into the air. This is the key to perfect timing and they should jump or extend when the ball passes through their eyes.

SHOOTING ARM

Checkpoint 3 is an extension of the shooting arm. The guide hand should no longer be in play and the arm should be extended from the elbow.

Players should push the ball out of the guide hand and extend the arm straight, keeping the wrist cocked until they have extended the arm. The force of the elbow extending straight will cause the wrist to flip through naturally so they should extend the arm straight at the basket. Just have them think "extend the elbow."

SHOT FINISH

Checkpoint 4 is the finish of the shot. The index finger should point down into the basket. The other fingers of the shooting hand should point straight up from the arm and wrist.

As the wrist was flipped through on checkpoint 3, the ball should roll off the ends of the player's fingers with their index finger being the last thing to touch the ball. This will give them follow-through with the ball—not under or over—and give them maximum touch control.

Pronation (good backspin) is needed and is accomplished by bringing the index finger down and the little finger slightly up. Let the index and middle finger be the last two things to touch the ball. The elbow should be above the level of the eyes at the conclusion of the release. This will give your players good arch.

If the elbow is below eye level, they will have a flat, straight-on shot. Have them keep the arm extended until the ball hits the rim. This lets them check final follow-through and improve their shooting.

There are 4 things to remember at this stage:

1. Index finger down in the basket.

2. Straight arm on the release.

3. Elbow above the eye level.

4. Leave the arm up until the ball hits the rim.

DRY SHOOTING DRILL

Dry shooting (shooting without the ball) is a must as a drill everyday! This way, your players are working on their technique and making every basket a mental picture. Once they've shot 25, go to flip-ups with the ball, shooting it straight up in the air and concentrating on your check points.

After 25, go to flip-ins. Have the player stand directly in front of the rim and shoot the ball, flipping it over the front of the rim with attention to the checkpoints. Once they have shot 25, have players begin moving back while using the checkpoints and sighting the target on the rim. Have your players concentrate on form and following the shot. They now have a solid, quick warm-up for shooting and are ready to work on the entire shooting arsenal.

It is merely a matter of practicing these techniques—500 to 1,000 made shots a day is recommended—to help them become good shooters. Have them concentrate on making 3 of every 5 shots and they'll become much better shooters!

–Rod Kirschner,
Head Men's Coach, Horton High School, Horton, Kan.

USE AN IMAGINARY PHONE BOOTH TO DEVELOP SUPER SHOTS

IN TODAY'S GAME, any technique that can simplify the game and improve player's skills in the process is greatly appreciated. One way to do this is have your players employ the imaginary phone booth.

Have shooters visualize themselves standing in a phone booth with the top removed. The object is to never touch the sides of the booth and avoid the "glass." Every coach realizes the importance of the shooting elbow in the success of a jump shot.

Proper elbow placement is probably the most important factor in accurately shooting a basketball. While standing in the booth, if the elbow flies out it will touch the "glass," which the shooter then realizes is a mistake.

The phone booth idea also eliminates floating and fading away by forcing the shooter to jump straight up and down during the shot. It also reminds shooters not to drift right or left while shooting.

Any of these four mistakes would not only lessen the shooter's accuracy, but would also force the player to "touch the glass."

UPWARD, OUTWARD

More importantly, the phone booth forces shooters to manipulate the ball upward and then outward during its release. Many young players push the ball rather than shoot it. The booth forces players to lift and then release the ball. (An up, up and away Superman-style motion). This results in more arch on the shot and more accurate shooting.

This up and out shooting motion also helps advanced players get in the air to shoot the ball over the defender.

The great aspect of the imaginary

phone booth is that it teaches players to visualize and analyze their technique—a skill that can enhance other parts of their game as well.

For instance, the "booth" can be used to eliminate cheap and costly fouls by defensive players.

CUT DOWN ON FOULS

W e often see post players in good defensive position (hands straight up) draw an unnecessary foul by reaching outward just as the shooter releases the ball. If the defender would imagine the shooter "in the booth" and reach straight up, these fouls would be eliminated.

Many times we see a great double-team nullified by an overly anxious defender trying to slap the ball out of an opponent's hands. If the defender would imagine the ball "in the booth" and wave their hands and arms outside the glass, these fouls would be cut in half.

Another nice aspect of the booth concept is the many key phrases and "trigger words" that can be used to remind players to use proper technique.

1. When a player is using improper elbow placement or failing to jump straight up and down, you can tell them to jump into the phone booth for a quick change.

2. When a defensive player is reaching out to attempt to block a shot or steal the ball, tell them to keep their fingers off the glass.

3. Perhaps the best trigger word is simply "Superman" to remind players to use the up, up and away shooting motion when releasing the ball.

Having used the phone booth with great success, any player who steps into the booth greatly enhances their chances of soaring to new basketball heights.

–Alvie King, Coach,
Milano High School,
Milano, Texas

SHOOTING TIPS FOR GUARDS AND WINGS

1. ELBOW JUMPERS, 2 PLAYERS

1 is the rebounder and the other the shooter. The shooter starts on an elbow and receives a pass from the rebounder. The shooter puts up a jump shot and, without waiting and watching, shuffles across the foul line to the opposite elbow to receive a pass from the rebounder.

This continues for 30 seconds to 1 minute before the players switch roles. This can be done from any place on the court, as long as you designate areas to shuffle and shoot from.

2. SHOOTING BUILD-UP

(For players who are weak shooters or have poor form):

Part I. Players lay on their back in a straight position on the floor. They have a ball in their shooting hand and practice holding the ball in proper shooting form, with the elbow lined up and ball on the fingertips (pad of hand).

The shooter fires the ball straight up and works on arm extension and follow through. If the ball comes back down to the hand area, then the arm and hand part of shooting is working well.

Part II. Have the player stand facing the basket (3 to 5 feet from the front of the rim). They should set themselves in proper shooting form with legs shoulder width apart and the dominant foot about a half length in front of the other. Keep the knees bent, butt down and the back slightly arched. The weak hand should be at the side while the shooting hand holding the ball should be elbow in, ball held with finger tips or pads at around head level and wrist cocked back.

Eyes should be focused on the rim. The player should go through their shooting motion but not jump, all the while being sure to follow through. Have them shoot the ball over the front of the rim and concentrate on form and extension. After doing this 25 times, have them move to the left and right side.s

3. 3-MAN SHOOTING

Have one rebounder, one outlet man and one shooter. They rotate every minute (shooter to rebounder to outlet). The rebounder picks up both makes and misses and passes to the outlet, who then makes a good pass to the shooter.

The shooter moves to a new spot after each shot and to areas that need work or which they shoot from.

4. 2-MINUTE 2 MAN SHOOTING

Have one shooter and one rebounder. The shooter takes shots from designated areas on the floor while the rebounder rebounds, making proper pivot and outlet pass to the shooter.

After each shot, the shooter moves to the next spot. Designate the spots where you want each shooter to shoot for 2 minutes before changing.

5. FREE-THROW LINE JUMP SHOT

The player sets up on free-throw line and takes a jump shot, follows the shot and rebounds any miss into an offensive rebound put back. After each rebound, change sides. This can also be done from other spots on the court.

6. PUMP, FAKE, JAB STEP

Cross Over Moves: Coach stands at one spot on the floor with the shooter in another. The shooter must V-cut to get open, flash to the coach, receive a pass from the coach, face up and make one of the moves mentioned above. He can shoot a jumper or drive off one of these moves. Have them work on a variety of moves.

7. HORSE CONTEST

Have your players use jump shot only and shoot nothing closer than 8 feet. They should take only legitimate game shots. Use 3 players at a time.

8. WOODY DRILL

Player stands under the basket and tosses a reverse spin pass to any area on the court. He goes to this toss, catches the ball, steps up for a jump stop, pivots to the basket and either shoots a jumper or makes another type of offensive move to the basket (one dribble jumper, baseline drive, power layup, etc.). This should be done at game speed.

–Peter Lasavage,
Akiba Hebrew Academy,
Merion, Pa.

"The only way to find your rhythm is by repetition. Do something 1,000 times and pretty soon you do it easily and gracefully."
— Adolph Rupp

SHOOTING (POST PLAYERS)

1. MIKAN DRILL

Using the power layup or baby hook, the player powers up for a layup on one side, catches the ball before it hits the floor and, in one motion slides and powers up the other side. Make sure your players use both right and left hands (depending on which side they're on) and keep the ball above their shoulders.

2. BAD PASS DRILL

Player stands 3 to 5 feet from the center of the rim. They face the basket and the coach stands on the free-throw line with a ball. The player must have their hands up, be relaxed and ready to pivot either way.

The coach slaps the ball and, in the same motion, throws a bad pass in the direction of the player (can be chest, bounce, overhead or rolled). The player must pivot move to the pass, gain control and take a shot without dribbling.

3. V-CUTTING IN POST

A. From box to foul line.

B. From low post to lane.

C. From low post to lane and roll to basket.

D. From opposite box to free-throw line and to the low post (to the ball).

All of these options start with the player away from the ball. Making the V-cut move mentioned previously, player jump stops, posts, receives a pass and uses a strong offensive move (drop step, turn around, baby hook or drive) to score.

4. PICK UP THE BALL AND SCORE

Have one ball on every block. Player 1 slides to a ball, picks it up and scores as player 2 rebounds and puts this ball back in its place. Player 1 slides to the other block and does the same thing. Continue for 30 seconds.

5. 2-ON-1 SHOOTING IN THE LANE

Two players stand in the lane about 5 to 7 feet from the basket. They face away with their hands up standing foot to foot. The third player has a ball and, standing face-to-face with the two defenders, puts up a shot.

The ball is rebounded and the players change positions, moving right to left. The two defenders don't do anything during the shot but play stationary defense with their hands straight up.

6. ROUGH HOUSE

Have your players stand in the lane (they can never leave the lane area). The coach on the free-throw line banks the ball off the backboard. The player who grabs the rebound tries to score against everyone else. Play continues until someone scores.

The coach then begins this drill over again. Each time a player scores, they may leave this drill. The first player who leaves the drill can go, while each player after this is given a suicide, lap, etc., until everyone is done. The last two players start on the blocks. We allow extra contact during this drill.

7. 2-ON-1 REBOUNDING

Three players stand in the lane and the coach throws the ball off the backboard. The player who grabs the rebound goes 1-on-2 in an attempt to score. When they do, the drill starts over.

–Peter Lasavage,
Akiba Hebrew Academy,
Merion, Pa.

---

12 Improvement Drills

INDIVIDUAL SHOOTING

1. FORM SHOOTING

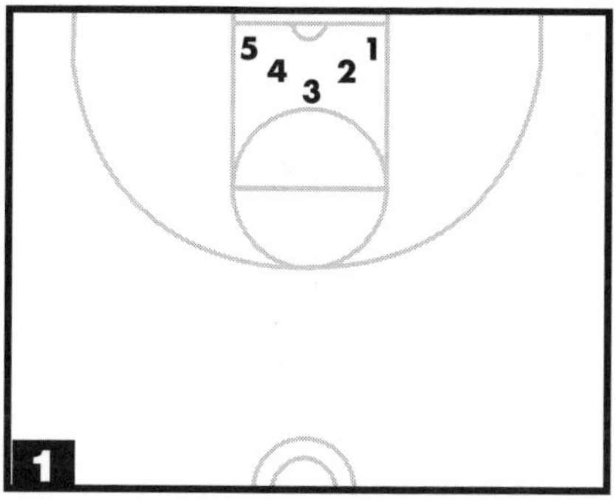

1. Players begin close to the basket.

2. Shoot 1-handed shots. Use proper form.

3. Knees are bent, extended up on toes, players release and follow through.

4. Players make 5 shots from each spot, take 1 step back and repeat.

2. SEVEN SPOT SHOOT AND FOLLOW (15 FEET)

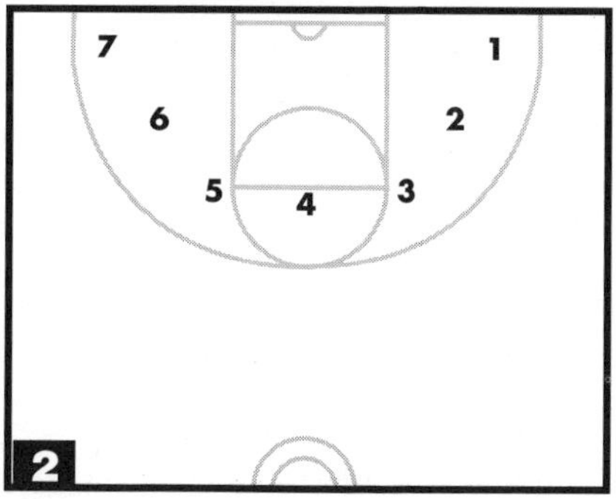

1. Shoot a jump shot from spot 1.

2. Have players follow the shot, dribble hard to spot 7, shoot the ball.

3. Follow, dribble hard to spot 1, shoot the ball.

4. Make 10 shots.

5. Repeat for spots 6 and 2, 5 and 3, and 4.

3. SEVEN SPOT SHOOT AND FOLLOW (3-POINT)

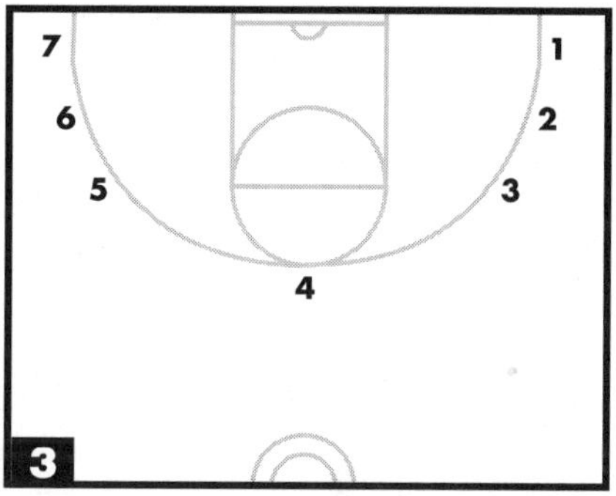

1. Repeat as with drill 2.

2. Step into your shot, elevate and release.

4. SQUARE-UP SHOOTING

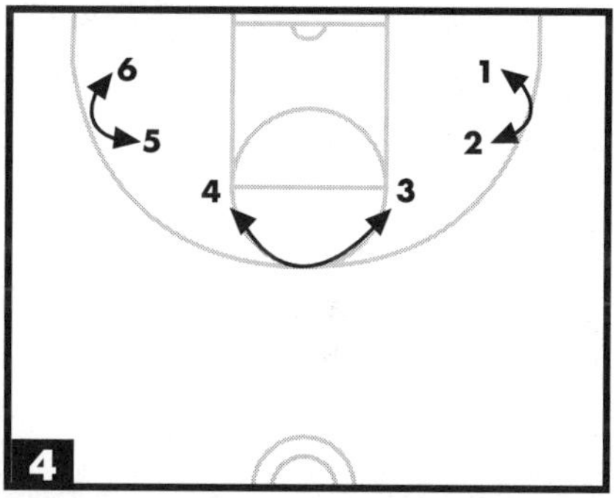

1. Begin at spot 1, flip the ball to spot 2.

2. Follow, get behind the ball, catch, elevate and shoot.

3. Make 10 shots, then move to spots 3 and 4 and repeat.

4. Finish by shooting in spots 5 and 6.

PARTNER SHOOTING

5. TWO MAN, SHOOT AND FOLLOW (15 FEET OR 3-POINT)

1. The drill begins with a good, crisp pass. Have players follow the pass.

2. The shooter catches the ball with knees bent, hands ready and the fingers

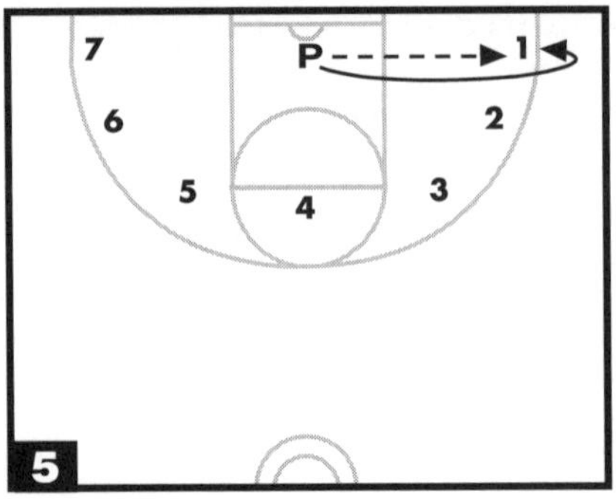

pointed up.

3. Catch and shoot the ball in a smooth motion.

4. Follow your shot, retrieve the ball and pass to the partner, who shoots.

5. Continue alternating until one person makes 5 shots.

6. Rotate and repeat for all 7 spots.

6. 2 MAN, SHOOT AND FOLLOW WITH CONTEST

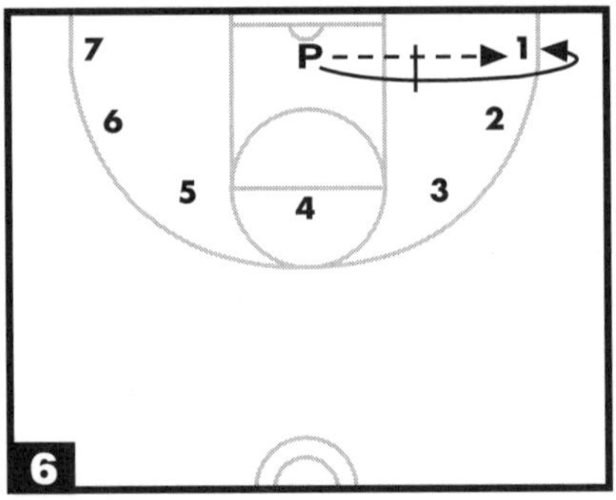

1. This drill is run as the previous drill.

2. Step into your shot as you catch ball.

3. Elevate and release the ball.

4. Shoot until one person has made 5 shots.

5. Rotate to the next spot and repeat for all 7 spots.

7. 2 MAN, SHOOT AND FOLLOW, SHOT FAKE

1. Drill is done as in 2 previous ones.

2. Catch the ball with knees bent and fingers pointed up.

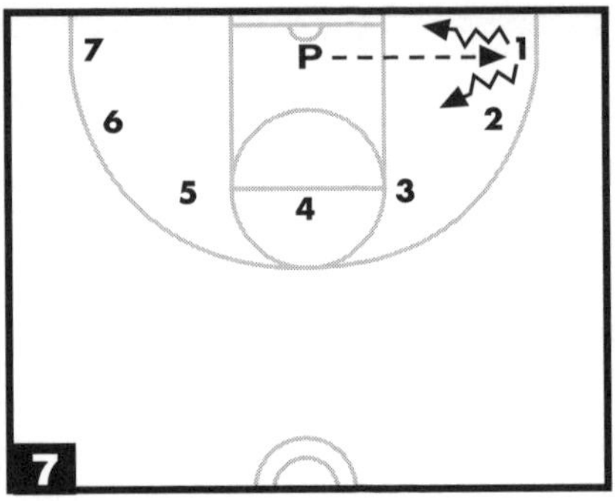

3. The defender follows the pass and contests the shot. Do not block.

4. The shooter gives a good shot fake and drives by body-to-body.

5. Take 1 or 2 dribbles, pull up and shoot a jumper.

6. Make 5 shots and rotate.

8. 2-MAN, SQUARE-UP (15 FEET OR 3 POINT)

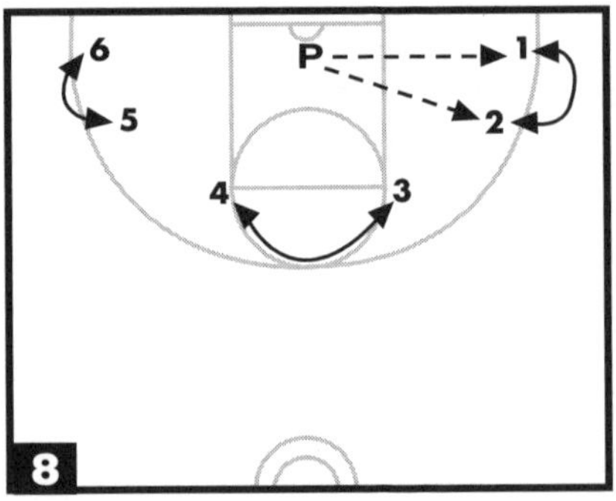

1. The shooter gets behind the pass with hands ready and fingers up.

2. The passer delivers the ball to the outside shoulder.

3. The shooter moves back and forth between the spots.

4. Shoot corner to wing (both sides) and elbow-to-elbow.

5. Make 7 shots, shoot 2 foul shots and rotate.

9. SHOTS ON THE MOVE (15 FEET OR 3-POINTS)

1. The shooter moves along the perimeter at game speed.

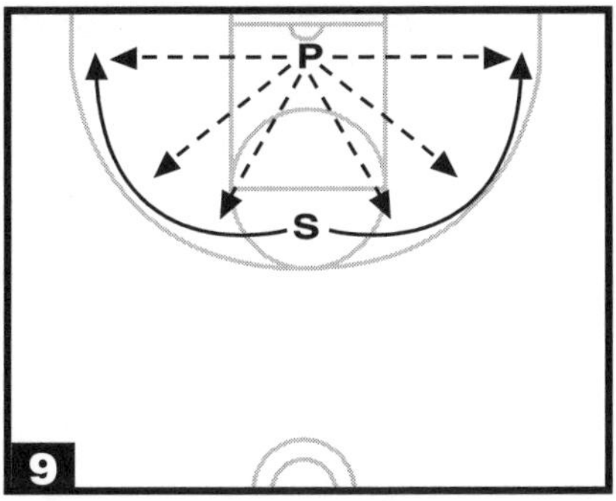

2. Passer delivers ball to outside shoulder.

3. The player should square, catch and shoot the ball.

4. Make 7 shots, shoot 2 foul shots and rotate.

5. This drill has 3 variations:
- A. Catch and shoot.
- B. Catch, shot fake, one or two dribbles same direction, jumper.
- C. Catch, shot fake, pull through opposite direction, 1 or 2 dribbles, jumper.

10. DRIBBLE SERIES, JUMPSHOTS (15 FEET OR 3-POINT)

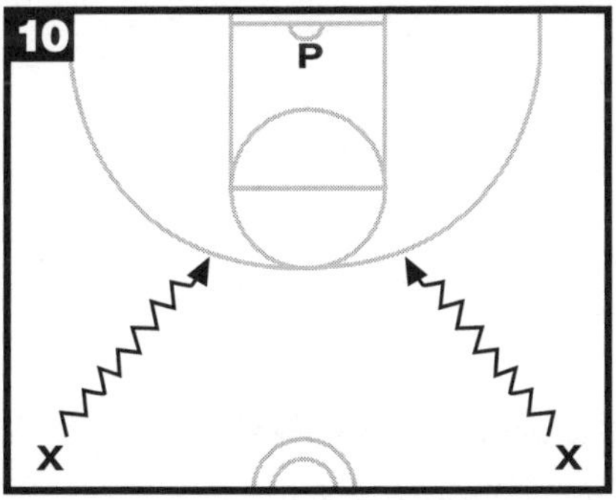

1. The shooter starts at half court and dribbles at game speed, drops weight down and shoots a pull-up jumpshot.

2. The non-shooter rebounds the ball and passes the ball to the shooter on the other side.

3. The shooter should begin dribbling with the right hand on the right side and the left hand on the left side.

4. Have your players use speed dribble, change of pace, inside-out, hard stutter and inside-out cross over.

3-MAN, 2-BALL SHOOTING

11. DRILL SET-UP

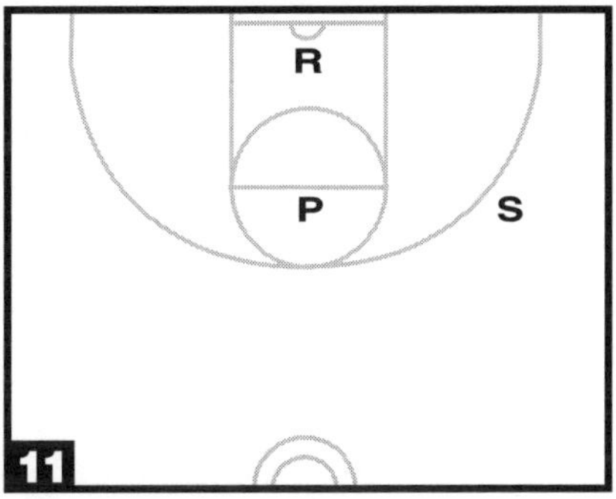

1. One player shoots, One player passes and one player rebounds.

2. Shooter puts up 7 shots, then becomes the rebounder.

3. The passer becomes the shooter and the rebounder becomes the passer.

12. DRILL VARIATIONS

1. 7 spot shooting (15 feet).

2. 7 spot shooting (3 point).

3. 5 spot shot fake.

4. Square-up shooting.

5. Shoot and follow.

–Ed Andrist,
Head Men's Coach,
University of Wisconsin —Stout,
Menomonie, Wis.

Shooting Contests

7 UP

Once a player makes a shot, the next player must duplicate the exact same shot. When a player misses a shot, they accumulate all the points from each contestant who made the same shot in a row preceding them.

Once a player accumulates more than 7 points, they're out of the drill. The player may have to explain the type of shot they're taking ahead of time.

BEAT THE PRO

Shoot every other shot left hand or right hand. Each time the player scores they get 2 points while each miss nets the pro 2 points. Play to whatever score has been predetermined. Options include different types of layups.

Another option is a "reverse gotcha" where the player shoots the layup first. If they miss, they must make the jumper from the elbow before the next person scores or the player is out.

STAR SHOT

Have your players start at the top of the key. Take a shot at the top of the key, rebound and go to the right baseline outside the key for the second shot. Rebound the second shot and go to the left elbow and shoot.

Rebound the third shot and go to the right elbow for a shot. Rebound the fourth shot and go to the left baseline outside the key and shoot. Rebound and start over again at the top of the key. Repeat the sequence until 55 seconds is up.

HOT SHOT

The player must start at the top of the key and can shoot anywhere on the floor for 55 seconds. The player must rebound their own shots. The only exception is the 1-point shot. The 1-point shot is taken from both sides of the basket. The 2-point shots are taken from just outside the key at the baseline. The 3-point shots are at each elbow and are equal distance on each baseline.

The 4-point shot is a free throw, while 5-point shots are behind the 3-point line. Points are earned based on where the shot was taken. The player with the most points is the winner.

–Daniel Brandel,
Head Boys' Coach,
Zoe Christian Academy,
Warren, Mich.

Skill Reinforcement Drill

(Drill time is 25 minutes)

RUN THE LINE

The player starts the drill by shooting a jump shot from the right side of the foul line and quickly moves to the left side of the foul line for a return pass from his or her teammate. The player should concentrate on catching the ball and flowing into the jump shot in a fluid motion. You need 1 or 2 rebounders.

RUN THE ANGLE LEFT

The same as above, but the player moves from the left elbow to the left baseline.

RUN THE ANGLE RIGHT

This is the same as the previous drill, but the player moves from the right elbow to the right baseline.

RAPID FIRE

From one spot the player shoots and two rebounders make sure the shooter has a ball as soon as they complete the shot. The player shoots as many baskets as possible in 55 seconds.

"X" SHOOTING DRILL

Begin with two coaches or managers having two balls, with each positioned opposite two lines of players. Line A of players is on the free-throw line extended. Line B of players is 3 feet from the key and on the baseline.

Players in line A cut low to the blocks and get a pass from the coach on the baseline. Players in line B cut high to the elbow extended on the opposite side.

Immediately after a player shoots, the next player in line cuts to receive a pass. Each player follows their shot, rebounds, dribbles out to the coach who passed them the ball and goes to the end of the opposite line.

Run this drill for 5 minutes before changing sides. Have a manager keep a record of shots made and try beating the previous score.

"I" SHOOTING DRILL

Players cut from the baseline to the elbow for a pass from the coaches, then square up and shoot, following their shots and dribbling out to the coaches who passed them the ball.

Players then change lines. The next player in each line cuts as soon as the players in front of them shoots. Intensity and hustle are stressed.

"V" SHOOTING DRILL

Players in two lines run a V-cut into the lane from the baseline and receive a pass from the coach. After taking the pass, they square up and shoot.

As soon as one player in each line shoots, the next player makes the same cut and follows the same procedure.

After shooting, players need to follow their shot, dribble out to the coach who passed them the ball and run to the end of the line.

STRAIGHT-LINE SHOOTING DRILL

Players form two lines at the free-throw line extended. Each line has 2 balls. The first player in line A starts the drill by cutting toward line B to receive the pass, then squares up and shoots, following their shot. The player dribbles over to the line of players that passed the ball.

The line B player who passed the ball cuts toward line A to receive a pass so they can shoot. The player in line A who passes the ball goes across to receive a pass from line B.

We like to have team competition in this drill. Our record is 126 baskets in 5 minutes.

FANTASY CHALLENGE

The player stands under the basket and tosses the ball with backspin toward the right corner within their shooting range. The player sprints in front of the ball so when it bounces he or she is facing the basket.

The player must turn as if they are receiving a pass from the wing or the top of the key area. Player catches the ball off the first bounce and pulls it back into the shooting pocket (directly above their shooting side hip) as quickly as possible.

The player shoots the ball and scores 1 point if they make the basket. The player continues moving from corner to corner until they reach a score of plus or minus 4. The winner from each baseline plays off at another designated spot directly in front of the basket.

PEPSI CHALLENGE

Break players into two teams. Each player gets 2 shots before returning to the end of the line. The first team to reach 11, 15 or 21 points wins. Players start with their feet outside the baseline on opposite sides *(diagram 1)*.

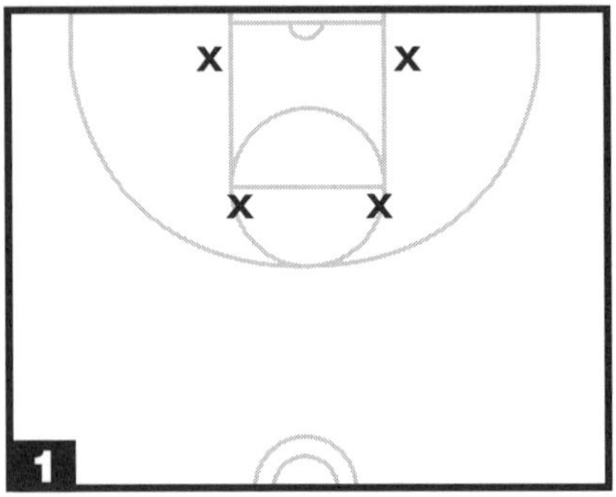

The second shot is from the elbow and shooters must rebound their own shot. Rotate starting positions until all shots have been taken. The baseline shot is a banker taken from the second slash mark.

HOT POTATO

Line up two players just outside the width of the backboard for a baseline shot. Shots taken must not hit the rim or backboard. The first player to sink 8 shots in a row wins.

Player 1 shoots until they miss, at which time player 2 starts. Player 2 gets two chances, picking up an extra chance off player 1's miss. Once player 2 misses twice, the ball returns to player 1 for 2 more tries. The drill continues until a player sinks 8 shots in a row.

3-2-1

In this drill, players shoot 3 shots from 5 different spots on the floor: 3-point shot, a 2-pointer from 15 to 17 feet and a layup (the drive starting at each of the 5 spots). Score 3 points for a 3-point shot and 2 points for the 15 to 17 foot shot, with 1 point for the layup. The maximum score per spot is 6 with a per-round score of 30. You can add a ball fake or a ball fake with a dribble.

–Daniel Brandel,
Head Boy's Coach,
Zoe Christian Academy,
Warren, Mich.

SHOOTING FOR SUCCESS IN THE OFF SEASON

I'VE SEEN MANY summer program workouts that specify an amount of shots each player should shoot. Shoot 100 3s, 20 jump shots, 20 jump shots off the dribble, 20 jump shots off a move, 20 bank shots and then 10 free throws.

These are very good, but we've taken shooting one step further. We now require our athletes to make a certain number of shots from each spot. This will give the good shooter a chance to speed through his workout, while the athlete who needs work will get more shots to try and improve.

SPOT SHOOTING

In practice, we used to shoot 25 shots from 5 spots with a partner. This was great, but our better shooter would finish more quickly than the rest of the team. Now we take shots from each spot for 2 minutes. Our better shooters get a lot of shots off, while other shooters are not pressured to shoot a certain number of shots.

Have players finish by setting a certain number of made shots in a row before they can get a drink. If they are shooting free throws, they might have to make 5 in a row before they can get a drink of water. This can be adjusted for each team or by position.

As a team we led the state of Indiana in team free-throw shooting one year at 78 percent. One year, my son shot 92.8 percent from the line for 155 of 167.

A typical summer shooting workout for our team might include:

1. Make 20 shots from each of 5 spots (2 baseline, 2 wing, 1 middle). Make 10 free throws.

2. Make 20 shots off the dribble. Make 10 free throws.

3. Make 20 shots off a move. Make 10 free throws.

4. Make 20 post moves. Make 10 free throws.

5. Make 20 drives to the basket and shoot. Make 10 free throws.

6. Make 20 3-point shots. Make 10 free throws.

7. Make 20 3-point shots off a move. Make 10 free throws.

8. Make 20 3-point shots off a pivot (go left and right). Make 10 free throws.

9. Make 20 3-point shots off a step-back move, (drive and step back). Make 10 free throws.

10. Make 20 3-point shots off a pass, with either a partner or a pass to yourself. Make 10 free throws.

Other drills you could add include: 20 bank shots, 20 bank 3s, 20 reverse layups or 20 hard layups. Use your imagination!

For you "stat" nuts: when your players have completed the workout, they will have made 100 free throws, 100 3-point shots and 180 other shots.

I've read where some kid over a summer took 40,000 shots.

How many did he make? If he made only 100, he's in trouble. The number made is more important, especially if they make them in a short amount of time. This means they make many more shots than they miss.

GIVE THEM A GOAL

Have your players pick a spot on the floor and make 5 shots in a row. This puts little individual pressure on the athlete and gives them a goal. This can be increased or decreased, depending on the player.

Do the same with free throws and have your players make 5 or 10 in a row before they quit. You can do this at the end of each different shot or at the end of the workout.

By all means change, modify and revise the workout as they go along. Do not follow this workout, or any workout for that matter, 7 days a week for 52 weeks a year.

Add variety and fun to make your players come back for more. Make it positive and motivating.

On an off day, we time our players to see how long it takes them to make 100 3-point shots with 1 ball and 1 rebounder. Our record is 6:58 to make 100 3-point shots.

This is only a shooting workout. We also have a ball handling, jump rope and a miscellaneous workout to add to and mix in with the shooting workout.

–Steve Drabyn,
Assistant Coach,
LaPorte High School,
LaPorte, Ind.

Change of Pace Drills

LUCKY "7" FREE THROW SHOOTING DRILL

Sometimes we need to work with individuals on post moves or work with guards on their outside moves.

That's when we let the players work on their free throw shooting skills using the lucky "7" drill. This makes a competition change of pace drill for our players. We put a chair under the basket and a manager sits with pen and paper. Their job is to keep score in the competition.

The object of the game is to be the last player shooting free throws without being eliminated from the competition.

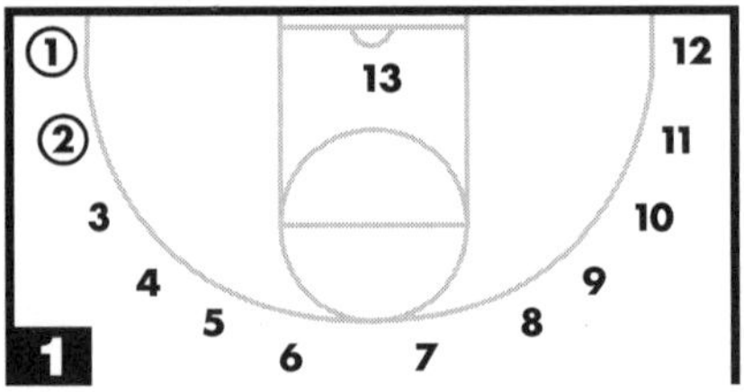

Each player lines up around the free-throw lane and shoots 1 free throw. If they make it, the next player shoots and if they miss, they get 1 point against them. If the third player misses the next free throw, nothing happens because the player in front of them did not make their free throw.

For example, if player 4 makes their free throw, 5 makes their free throw and 6 misses their free throw they then get 2 points against them. When players accumulate 7 points they are eliminated. If 7 free throws are made in a row, then the next player to miss is out of the competition.

3-POINT SHOOTING COMPETITION DRILL

We use this drill at the end of practice, before a game day or as a change of pace. This breaks up the practice routine and the players really enjoy this drill because we usually give away 3 sodas. The last 5 players have to dribble 2 basketballs around the gym with dribble glasses on.

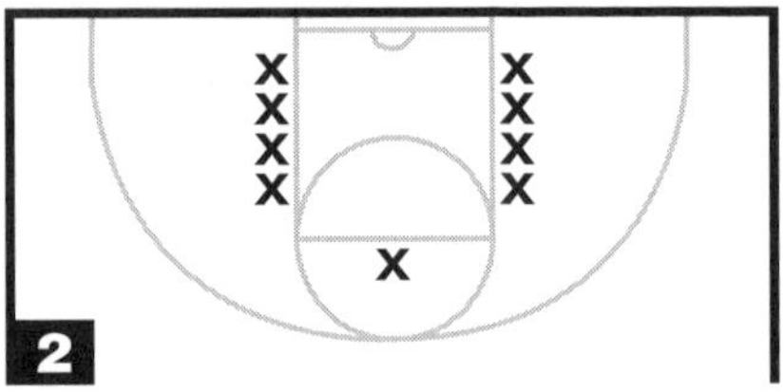

Players 1 and 2 start out with a basketball. 1 shoots first and if they make it from 3-point range they stay in their spot. If they hit the rim they remain in the spot. If they shoot an air ball, however, they head to the middle of the lane and become the rebounder in last place.

Player 13, who is the last player, becomes the number 1 player and shoots from there, following the same rules we have gone over. Next, player 2 shoots and then 3, etc. We usually go around the circle 5 rounds to give each player a chance to win the soda.

The last player can only get out of last place if an air ball is shot, upon which they would trade places with that shooter or—when his turn comes up—get a shot from the #12 spot on the floor. If they make it, they would move up to the last player who made a shot and player #12 would slide down to last place. Remember that if a player makes a shot, they move up to the closest spot to the #1 position that's open.

–Bill Kunze, Coach,
Duluth East High School,
Duluth, Minn.

Chapter 4

DEFENSE & REBOUNDING

1, 3, 1 TRAPPING ZONE

DRILLS TO PERFECT THE DEFENSE

If coaches can make their players believe in this zone, any opponent is sure to have trouble beating it and it will quickly gain favor with players. But University of Kentucky coach Joe Hall was right when he said, "Played without total devotion, it is the worst defense."

Like any defense, coaches must sell this zone with its calculated risks to their players.

The following are some drills to teach and perfect the moves and the synchronization of the defense.

DIAGRAM 1: WINGMAN, BACKMAN

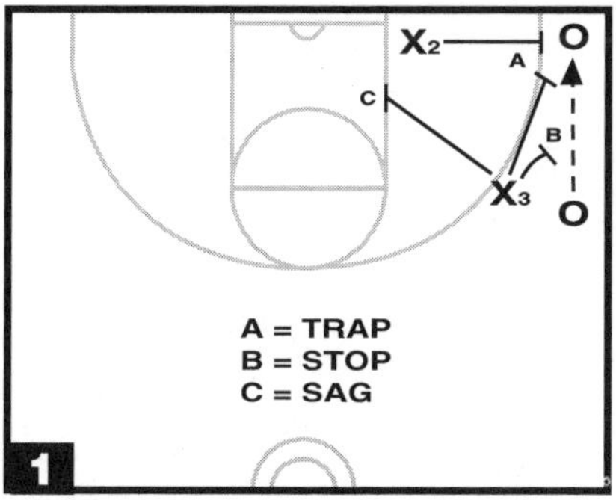

Forward passes to the corner. The moment the ball leaves their hands, the baseline defender (X2) jumps to the corner (not earlier, since this leaves the low post wide open; not too late either as they must stop the shot from the corner).

The wing defender (X3) turns and can do one of three things (depending on the variation we are teaching: trap in the corner, sag to the paint or stop the return/pass to the wing). Run the drill on both the left and right side.

DIAGRAM 2: WINGMAN, WINGMAN, BACKMAN

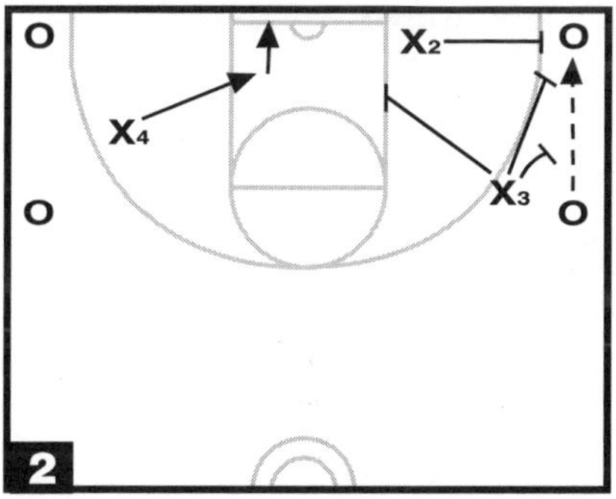

This is the same drill as 1, but now the weak side wingman (X4) is put in. The offense is in a shell position. No passes from corner to corner.

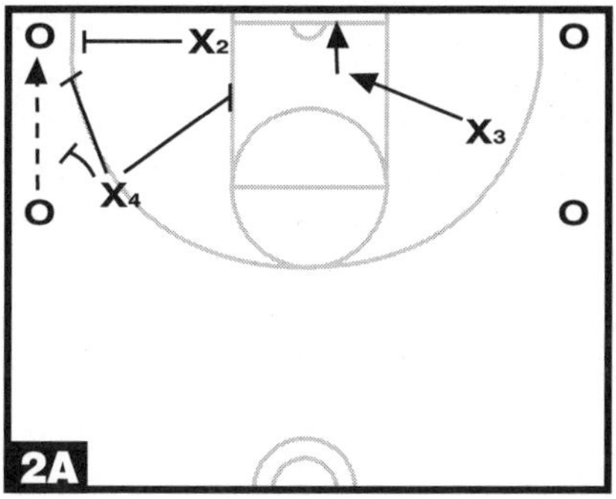

DIAGRAM 3: WINGMAN, TOPMAN, WINGMAN

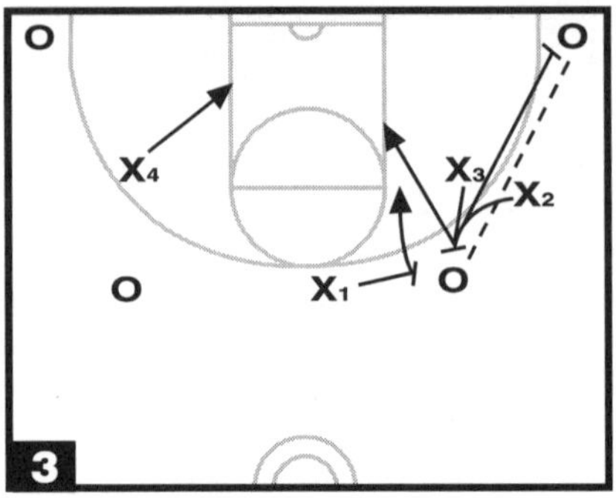

Offense is in shell position (two guards, two corner men and no forwards). The corner men are not active. The other two offensive players may try to drive.

DIAGRAM 4: TOPMAN, MIDDLEMAN, BASELINE MAN (I-DRILL)

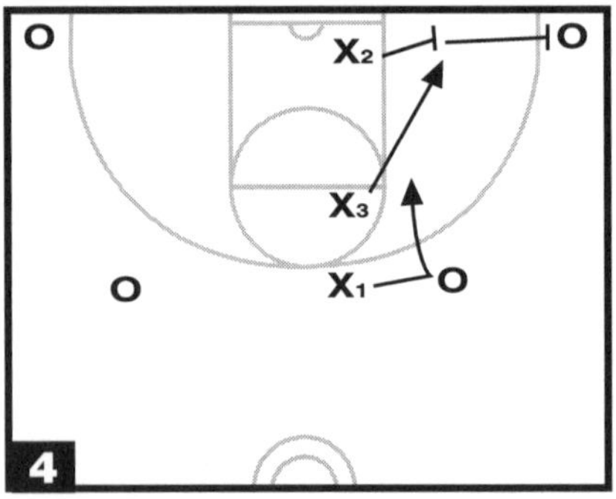

Same position as in diagram C for the offense. The three defenders adapt their position to the ball (X3 goes low when X2 goes to the corner). Played on left and right side. Later, the opposite offensive players may flash to the ball.

DIAGRAM 5: POINTMAN DRILL

Use four offensive players in a "big shell" (two guards and two forwards) and a big post player. X1 allows only bounce or lob passes between the two guards and intercepts passes from the wing to the high post.

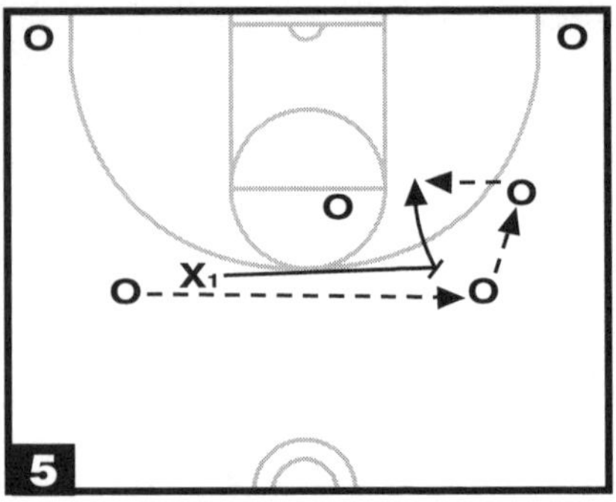

DIAGRAM 6: MIDDLEMAN DRILL

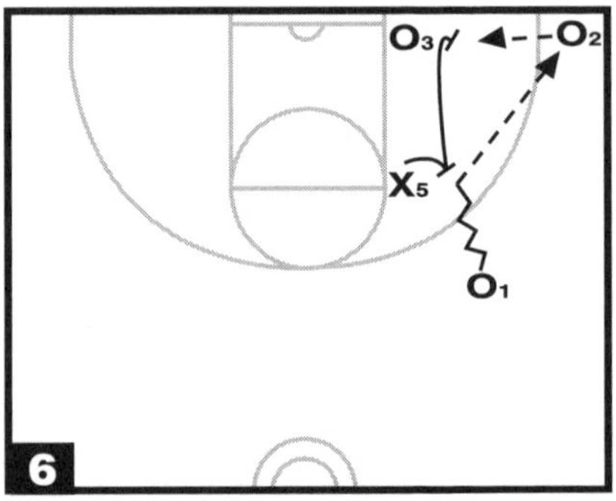

If there is penetration from the top, the middleman must stop the driver. There are three offensive players. As the two baseline players are stationary, the top man drives. When X5 attacks them, they pass to the corner,who immediately passes to the low post. X5 jumps in front of the low post as soon as the ball leaves the hands of the driver and tries to intercept the ball. Use on both the left and right sides.

DIAGRAM 7: MIDDLEMAN DRILL

Nearly the same drill as 6, but even more difficult. We now have four offensive men: the top man can drive or pass to the high post. X5 denies the pass from the guard to the high post, then stops the dribbler and immediately jumps in front of the low post. When attacked, O1 passes to the wing, O2, who immediately passes to the low post. 2 may not

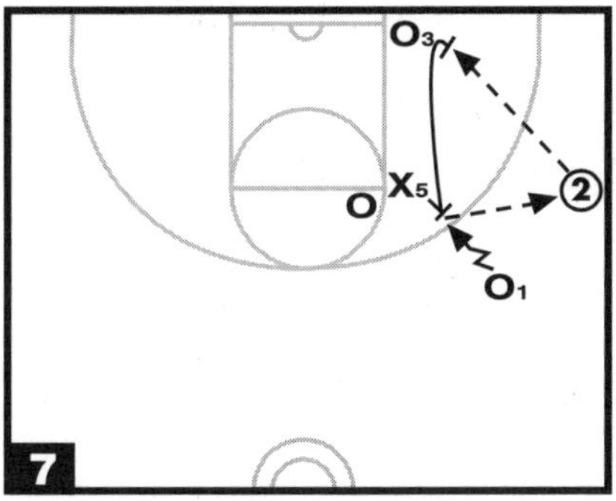

pass to the high post. High post, low post and wing are stationary.

Why must 2 immediately pass to the low post? To make X5 believe that in a real game they are able to stop the driver and then stop (or intercept) the pass.

DIAGRAM 8: DIAMOND TRAPPING DRILL— POINTMAN, TWO WINGMAN, BACKMAN

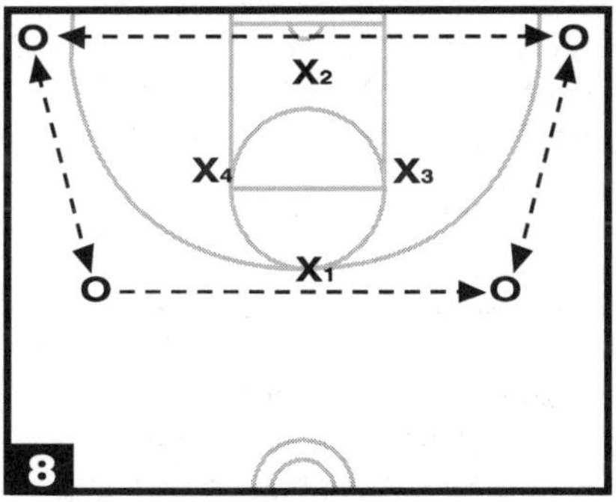

In this shell drill, the offensive players try to penetrate with the ball (they can later drive or shoot when totally open). The defenders slow down the passes (they have at least one hand in the passing lane). The defenders position themselves according to the command: trap, sag or stop.

DIAGRAM 9: TRAINING THE ZONE

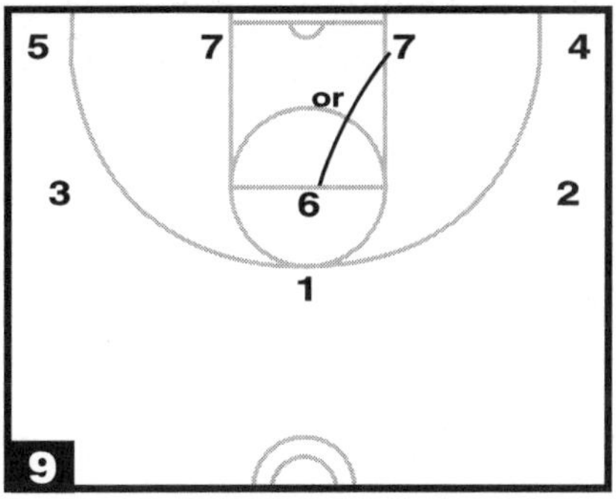

Once the players know their positions, make it more difficult for them by pitting 7 offensive players against them in these positions.

DIAGRAM 10: TRAINING THE ZONE

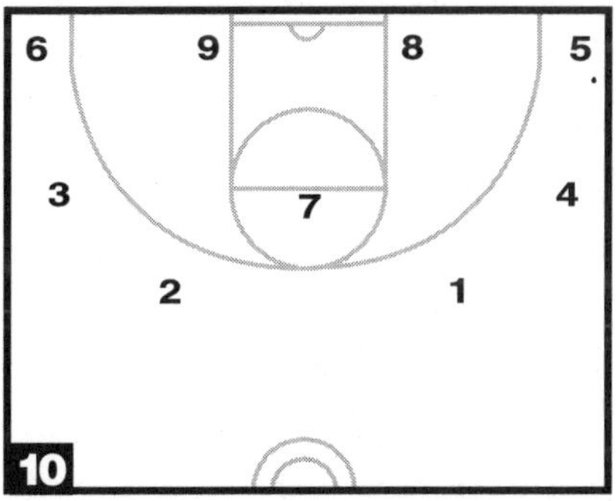

Put 9 offensive men in these positions against the zone defense. In both drills, the defense has to stop only the outside shot of the open player. Later on, the offense can shoot, drive and cut!

–Wim Cluytens,
Head Men's Coach,
Mechelen, Belgium

Team Defensive, Mental Quickness Drill

IT'S NO SECRET that all great teams are sound defensively. They have developed good defensive habits through drills. Every coach has their favorite team defensive drills such as the 6-on-4, 5-on-4, 4-on-4 open post, 5-on-5 change and shell drills.

The defensive change drill is an excellent way to combine and work on these drills while also developing mental quickness in your players.

QUICKNESS AS A COMMODITY

Indiana coach Bobby Knight has said that the mental is to the physical as four is to one. Quickness is one of the most valuable commodities a player can possess. One of the most effective ways to develop that quickness is by improving a player's mental quickness.

A player who is mentally sharp–someone who can recognize, anticipate and act quickly–is a very good player. This drill aids in developing that player.

To run the drill, divide players into two teams. Next, think of your favorite team defensive drills and choose three of them for the drill (more can be added if your player's mental capabilities allow it).

Run the drill just as you would any other team defensive drill except, after each possession, the coach will call out the name of a different drill (one of the three). The players must quickly adjust and begin the new drill. If it takes any longer than 7 seconds to run, it's too slow.

The coach can switch drills on every possession or every other one by calling out the name of the drill.

For example, say you choose the 4-on-4 open post, 5-on-4, and 6-on-4 drills. the 4-on4 open post could be the first drill used. After either a turnover, a defensive rebound and outlet or a made basket, call out a different drill.

Calling out a new drill after each possession makes your players think and react quickly to new situations.

MIX IT UP

The key to using these drills is to not become predictable in calling the drills, as well as demanding that it take no longer that 7 seconds to begin the new drill.

This drill can also be turned into a competition between the two teams by giving a point for every defensive stop and subtracting a point for every basket scored on the defense. You can also subtract points for giving up offensive rebounds.

This drill has many dividends, as it will improve defensive skills and habits, mental quickness and communication. Communication will improve because the players must tell each other who is in the drill (players sub themselves) where they should be stationed in the drill and who is guarding whom.

The defensive change drill can improve your team's defensive ability. Adapt it to your personal style and give it a shot.

–Michael McBride,
Assistant Coach, Marian College,
Indianapolis, Ind.

DEFENSIVE "SHELL DRILL"

OUR SHELL DRILL is designed to cover all the various offensive concepts an opposing offense could possibly throw at us. The drill is on a time basis with 4-player teams working the drill.

Each 4-man group goes from these stations:

A. The "defensive" station.

B. A "dummy offense" station.

C. A "watching and learning" station.

D. An "offensive" station. Then back to the "defensive station."

In the "defensive" station, each group of defenders should rotate from the high spots to the lower spots before switching to the "offensive" station. Three groups (four players each) can easily and effectively benefit from the shell drill also. The fourth station can be omitted.

Each player involved in the "watching and learning" station (C) has a basketball. If the ball in the shell drill is deflected or a bad pass goes out of bounds, the "learner" nearest the loose ball throws their ball in to keep the drill moving. We do not want any interruptions.

If there is a fourth group (D), that group is shooting on the side court or working on a designated offensive technique. Each group rotates from one station to the next station every 1 or 2 minutes. The drill should be fast-moving, so every player is involved and kept busy. Every player should be watching and listening, learning and improving (Diagram 1).

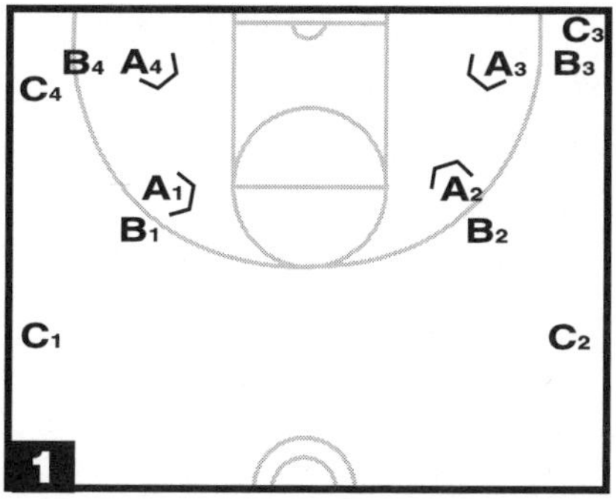

At the beginning of the season, we try to progressively cover all the various defensive scenarios. Once the games begin, we narrow down the topics to be covered for that particular game or week with the concepts that we expect our opponents to utilize in their offensive schemes.

DEFENSE IS CRITICAL

We stress to our players how important defense is when guarding the ball, but that the majority of their defensive time and effort will be spent on guarding someone who does not have the ball.

Their man might be without the ball in the post area, in the perimeter close ("one pass away") to the ball, or even on the perimeter farther from the ball ("two or more perimeter passes away").

The more support that "off-the-ball defenders" can provide to their teammate, who is an "on-the-ball defender," the more pressure the 'on-the-ball defender' can provide to help neutralize the opposing offensive man's (with the ball) three main offensive threats:

1. Shooting.

2. Dribbling and penetrating to the basket.

3. Passing the ball.

The more pressure that can be applied to the ball handler, the more effective your overall team defense will be. The more support the "on-the-ball defender" receives from his four defensive teammates, the more pressure that player can provide. Knowing how to correctly play defense in all of these situations is a must for every defender.

We play a "ball-you-man" flat triangle positioning of all of our "off-the-ball" defenders. We stress that the "off-the-ball" defenders should always see the ball and their man. If a vision sacrifice is to be made, players should give up sight of the ball momentarily before adjusting to a new (flat triangle) position in order to peripherally see both the ball and the man.

Our "off-ball" defenders should play in a "pistol stance" (pointing to and also seeing the ball and their man), straddling one of the two lines of tape in the lane. Which line they straddle depends on whether the ball is above or below the (imaginary) free throw line extended. In all instances, we play one step off the passing line (to form the flat triangle) with the ball side arm and leg slightly forward.

If a defender is guarding a man that's 2 feet or more perimeter passes away from the ball (in Diagram 2, 4 is on the "helpside forward" who is 2 or more perimeter passes away from the ball; while 1 is the "helpside guard" who is 2 or more perimeter passes away from the ball, If his man is above the free-throw line extended), that "off-ball" defender should be straddling one of the two lines in a "pistol stance"—seeing the ball and the man.

If the ball is below the free-throw line extended (which is closer to the basket and therefore more of a threat to our defensive team), that defender should be 1 step ball side.

This means the off-ball defender has sagged off their man and sloughed off toward the ball. 2 is the defender who is guarding a player that's 1 perimeter pass away. In this example, 3 is the ball defender and is "fanning" the dribbler toward the baseline hash mark. Once there, they could receive help from 4 rotating over as 1 rotates down *(diagram 2)*.

If the ball is above the free-throw line extended, the off-ball defender should stay one step man side. This means the off-ball defender (4) still sags off to help their defensive teammates, but not as much. So 4 stays one step man side while 3 and 1 are both perimeter defenders who are 1 pass away from the ball.

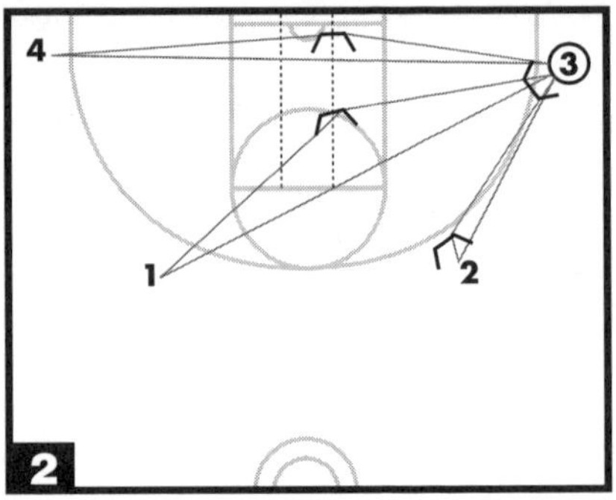

2

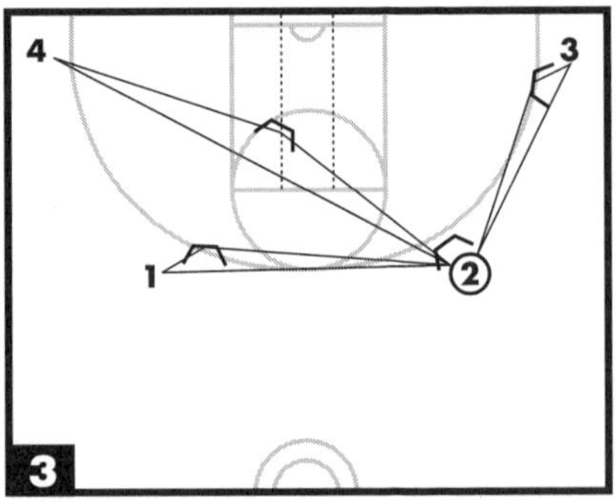

3

Obviously, 2 is the ball defender who is shading or fanning the ball towards the sideline and, ultimately, the baseline *(diagram 3)*.

"LONG ARM" TECHNIQUE

When our off-the-ball defenders are guarding someone in the ball side post (5) or on the perimeter just 1 pass away (2), we change our stance and technique. We call the defender's ball side arm their "long arm." Stress constantly the value and importance of using the "long arm" to deny passes to their man, especially when they become a 1-pass away threat in the post or the perimeter area. The palm of the "long arm" should be out and the thumb pointing downward. The defenders (in this case, 5 and 2) should be looking down their "long arm" in order to see both the ball and their man.

We emphasize how important the "pistol stance" is when defending off the ball. We want our off-ball defenders (4 and 1) to be off their man for two main reasons:

1. To buy themselves some reaction time to react to their opponent's offensive moves.

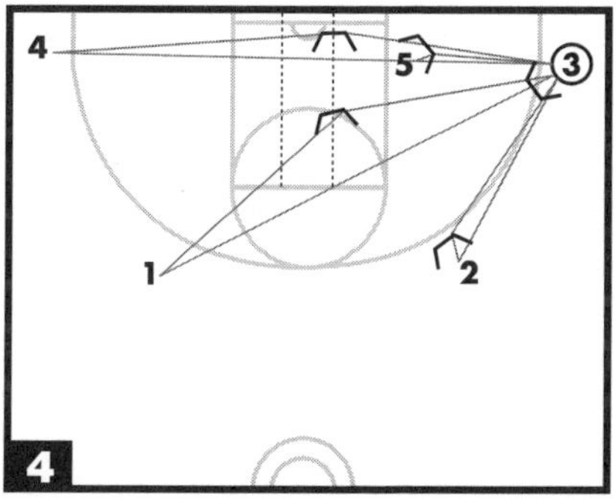

4

2. To be closer to the basketball and able to help more quickly *(diagram 4).*

Any time there is movement of the ball and/or movement by their man, that defender should quickly readjust to form the new correct "ball-you-man flat triangle." The coaching staff constantly yells "Jump to the ball" after every pass by the offense during the shell drill.

We try to instill in our defensive players that great defense can be achieved with the following:

Heart.
Guts.
Proper Stance.
Proper Location.
Positioning.
Proper Technique.

Lay down tape on the gym floor to assist both the coaching staff in teaching and coaching the players and for every player to thoroughly learn the

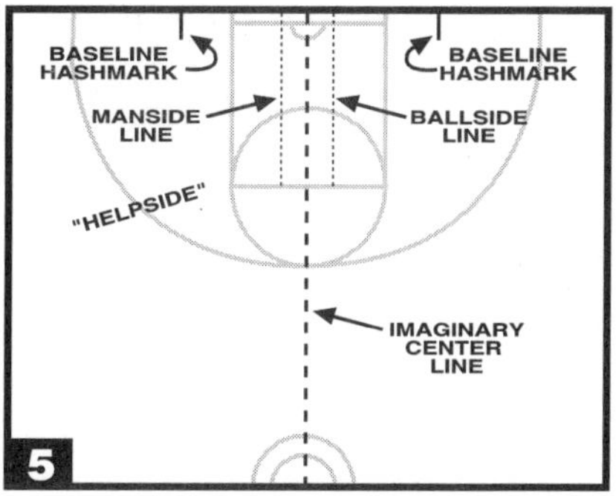

5

proper positioning in every possible offensive scenario.

The tape is used in learning and reinforcing the proper positioning of each defensive basketball player. There are two strips of tape that we lay down for each free throw lane, each 3 feet on both sides of the imaginary center line of the lane. *(diagram 5).*

The tape on the baseline is located on each side of the free-throw lane, 3 feet outside of the lane on the baseline. We call them our defensive "baseline hash marks." These serve as visual clues to both our ball defenders and off-the-ball defenders *(diagram 5).*

These 4 strips of tape serve as a tremendous teaching tool for the coaching staff, as well as a great visual guide for all defensive players involved in practice and games.

During videotape sessions, it's easy to spot players who are positioned correctly, as well as those who have improperly positioned themselves. Players can easily critique themselves during videotape sessions, as well as see their own correct positioning when it happens during practice or in games.

We have 6 baskets with tape laid out in the free throw lanes of each, as well as on the baselines. The tape serves as an effective teaching aid for our players' individual defensive positioning, regardless of where the ball or their specific offensive man is located.

START SLOWLY

When initially teaching the team defense, start slowly with the positioning segment, so each defender can learn the proper location/position and the proper stance they should be in while the ball is positioned in various areas of the court. Offensive players are limited to a 3-foot area of movement. They also must catch the ball and hold it for 2 counts but not try to beat the defense.

Since there's a lot of teaching and learning involved, we periodically yell "freeze" to have everyone check themselves and their teammates for the proper positioning, location, stance and techniques. Make sure every player learns all 4 defensive perimeter positions and the ball side and weak side low post positions.

The baseline hash mark tape serves as a guide for the ball defender to ideally fan the ball to that specific spot and shut the ball down by themselves.

If necessary, we want our help side defenders to rotate over on a baseline drive, but we don't want them to rotate over too soon, too late or too far out.

If and when the ball defender needs help on the baseline, they must call out for help. The help side forward rotates over no further than the ball side baseline hash mark, while the help side guard rotates down to pick up their new man.

When the dribble is killed in this area, it's one of the worst spots a "killed offensive dribbler" can end up in. An offensive player has 3 offensive threats—shooting, dribbling and passing.

The ball is behind the basket to make the shot more difficult. On the baseline, the dribbler has lost half of their 360 degrees they had to attack. If they've killed their dribble, they've also lost that threat.

The backboard, rim, net and defender(s) should block 90 degrees of their passing angle possibilities, with the remaining 90 degrees retreating away from their basket so their passing threats are greatly diminished.

Therefore, the offenses' three threats of shooting, dribbling and passing have been greatly weakened. They'll have a difficult shot, their dribbling area will have shrunk and their passing angles have been cut in half.

ADDING NEW ELEMENTS

After your players have mastered the elementary phase, move onto the more sophisticated offensive concepts. Have the defense show it can intercept the pass, but let all passes go through.

It forces the offensive players to concentrate on passing and catching the ball, while showing the defenders what they need to do in order to make interceptions. You can also place restrictions on what type of passes must be made to develop the offensive players passing skills.

The particular offensive scenarios that we've accumulated from every offense we've ever been exposed to over the years are defended by the following breakdown situations:

"OFFENSIVE CONCEPTS, SCENARIOS"

1. "Positioning."
2. Vs. "give-n-go" cuts.
3. Vs. "back door" cuts.
4. Vs. "clearouts."
5. Vs. "skip passes."
6. Vs. "killed dribble."
7. Vs. "on-the-ball" screens.
8. Vs. "off-the-ball" down screens.
9. Vs. "off-the-ball" cross screens.
10. Vs. "off-the-ball" back screens.
11. Vs. "off-the-ball" flex back screens.
12. Vs. "off-the-ball" shuffle-cut back screens.

13. Vs. "shuffle-cut" action.

14. Vs. "wheel-cut" action.

15. Vs. "scissor-cut" action off of post.

16. Vs. UCLA rub-off back screens.

17. Vs. "off-the-ball" pin screens.

18. Vs. "off-the-ball" stagger screens.

19. Vs. "off-the-ball" lane exchange screens.

20. Vs. "flash post" action.

21. Vs. "help-n-recover" (G to G).

22. Vs. "help-n-recover" (G to F).

23. Vs. "help-n-recover: (G to C).

24. Vs. "baseline drives."

25. Boxouts on a shooter.

26. Boxouts on "ball side."

27. Boxouts on "help side."

28. Vs. "skip passes."

29. Vs. "super star" post or perimeter player.

30. Late game situations and fouling when behind or ahead."

31. Vs. "flex" dummy offense.

32. Vs. "passing game" dummy offense.

33. Vs. "triangle power game" dummy offense.

34. Vs. "wide" (give-n-go and/or slash cut) offense.

35. Transition from defense to secondary break(s) from misses only.

36. Transition from defense to secondary break(s) from opponents' turnovers.

37. Transition from defense to secondary break(s) from opponents' mades only.

38. Transition from defense to press offense(s) to secondary break(s) after opponents "made basket" and then a "press." This includes moving from a half-court offense to a defensive transition and into a specified shell drill with a defensive point of emphasis.

We preach to our players proper stance, proper location, positioning, proper technique, intensity and that desire equals defensive success.

Offense wins games, but defense wins championships.

You can have an off night on offense, but you should never have an off night on defense. Defensive success is the mainstay of a solid basketball team and a winning program.

–John Kimble,
Head Men's Coach,
Crestview High School,
Crestview, Fla.

"When a gifted team dedicates itself to unselfish trust and combines instinct with boldness and effort, it is ready to climb to the top."

2-Line Series

THIS IS AN intense defensive drill that's an excellent way to teach some parts of our man-to-man defense. We call it our "2-Line Series" and except for the first couple of practices that we run it, we generally only spend 10 minutes executing the drill. As with all defensive drills, we would rather have it be short and intense.

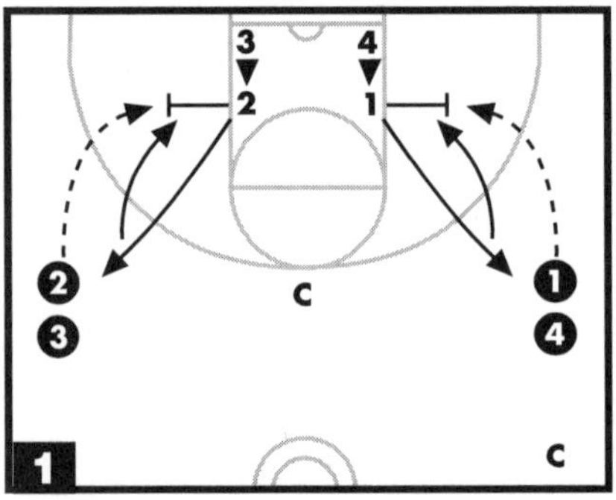

This 2-line series will incorporate closeouts from the helpside, pressure on the ball, forcing the dribble to the outside, help defense on penetration, 1 pass away denial and live action to incorporate all the man-to-man defensive principles that you choose to teach.

Start the drill with two equal lines on the baseline and two players on each wing with a ball for each player. The coach stands on top as the first two players in each line step up to the block.

The coach says "Go" and the first two defenders cross and close out to the opposite wing while the next two defenders in line step up to the block and are now the help side defenders.

EXECUTING THE CLOSEOUT

On the closeout, we want players to closeout short (play the shot, think and drive) with weight back, arms parallel and active hands. In terms of the footwork, we teach the stutter step on the closeout.

After the defender closes out under control, players apply tremendous pressure on the ball, forcing it to be dribbled outside (defensively, we don't allow the ball to be dribbled to the middle of the floor).

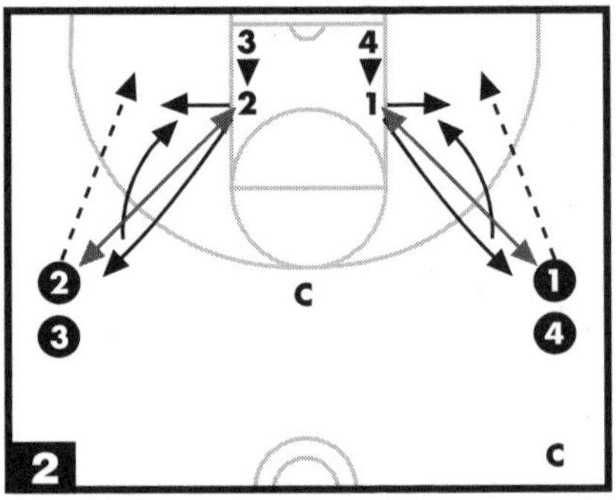

As the ball is being dribbled to the outside, you should count on the help defender to step out and stop penetration. As the offensive player is picking up their dribble, the defender on the ball is in their face yelling "dead" and the help defender retreats back to the block area.

Play continues until the whistle blows and the rotation continues when the coach says "go." The help defenders will cross and closeout.

The next two players in line step up to the block for help side, while the player that was on defense goes to the wing for offense and the offensive player goes to the end of the line for defense.

After every player has gone through each line once, start the second drill. Starting on the block, the defensive player pretends to be guarding someone who is trying to get open on the wing.

The defender will be in a denial stance and will deny out to the ball and back to the block twice (make them go hard on the denial, hand in the passing lane, thumb to the floor, looking over the shoulder to see the coach on top).

On the third time to the wing, players closeout on the ball, force the dribble outside and the next player in line steps up to the block for help side.

After the dribble is stopped and picked up, the help defender executes the denial slides. The previous offensive player goes to the end of the defensive line and the defensive player goes to the wing line. Have each player go through each line at least once.

BLOCKING FROM THE HELP SIDE

The third part of the drill has players blocking out from the help side. One coach stands on top with another on the baseline with the ball. When the coach on top gets the pass

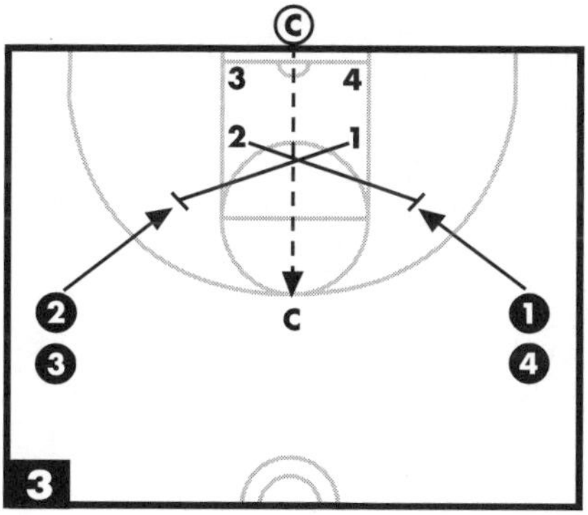

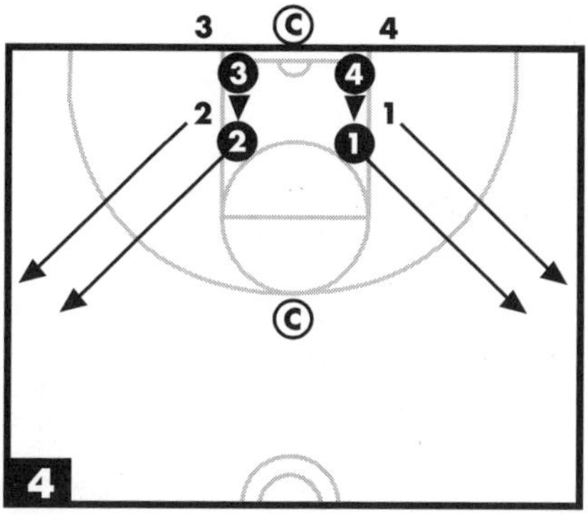

from the baseline, they will catch and shoot. The two defenders on the block will cross, closeout, blockout.

Our philosophy on blockouts is simple–players prevent their man from getting the ball! After the coach shoots and players blockout, blow the whistle when the ball bounces more than once.

The final part of the drill is basically 2-on-2 live. A coach will stand on top with the ball while all the players are on the baseline in two equal lines. The first two in each line step up to the block, one on offense and one on defense.

Players must go hard to deny the ball to the wing (to prevent an obvious backcut, have the next two players in line step up to the block for help side. Once the ball is entered, have the help step off the court so we can play a 2-on-2 game).

When the ball enters, players must put tremendous pressure on the ball, forcing the dribble to the outside while helpside sprints to get a foot on the ball side lane.

The players again go live and play until the whistle blows. This is a great way to close the drill because you can emphasize everything (deny one pass away, force outside, helpside, ball pressure, blockouts, etc.) that have been taught about man-to-man defense.

A couple of suggestions to make the 2- Line Series even better and more intense: Have players mimic and talk in line. Everyone mimics the helpside defender during the drills. This way you get even more repetitions. Make everyone in line talk and talk loud, calling out the position of the defender.

If the ball is dribbled to the middle, have the two defenders do 5 push ups.

–Shawn Neary,
Head Men's Coach,
Miles Community College,
Miles City, Mont.

Get Tough Drills

A COMMON FACTOR of successful teams is the willingness of players to commit to aggressive, physical play.

Our coaching staff has set rules regarding specific game situations. For instance, a man-to-man defensive rule is to chuck (bump) your player when they flash from the weak side to the ball.

A post player must create contact with a post defender before establishing on the low post for a ball entry. These are just two of the coaching mandates involving contact which our kids are required to execute.

While coaching high school girls, the young women may not have the willingness to play a contact game. Many players have been discouraged by recreational league coaches to avoid being overly aggressive. Some have even been chastised or penalized for wrongly perceived "rough play."

To alleviate the practice of passive basketball, not only do we define contact rules for situational play, but we also initiate "get tough drills" as a big part of our pre-season practice. These drills are commonly bound by two extreme behaviors:

1. Overaggressive play.

2. Physical contact (the concept of fouling is non-existent).

FOUR CORNERS LOW POST DRILL (DIAGRAM 1)

This is a continuous drill utilizing all four corners of half-court. Players are evenly divided, with balls for all players in the left corner. Players replace to the line they passed to.

X1 passes across the court to X2 and immediately establishes defensive position between X3 and the ball side low post block. X2 passes to the corner,

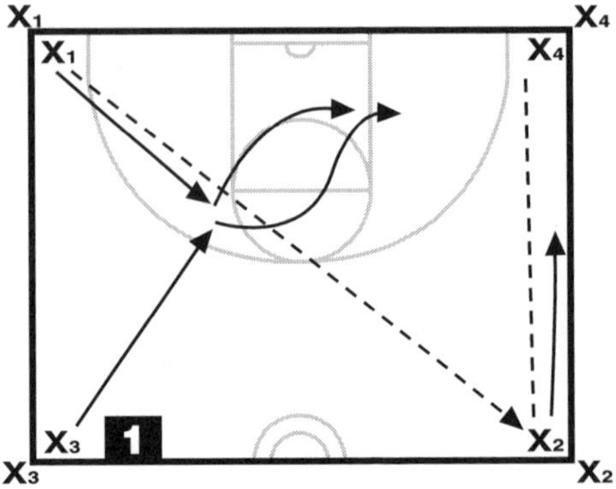

X4, and assumes a wing position. X3 attempts to establish low post position.

X1 must adjust X3's route by chucking X3. Once X3 assumes low post position, X1 three-quarter denies the entry from X4 (corner) or X3 (wing). X3 constantly makes contact with X1 while sealing for the entry. This is a no-foul, do what you must drill.

PERSON TO PERSON DENIAL, STEAL, DEFEND DRILL (DIAGRAM 2)

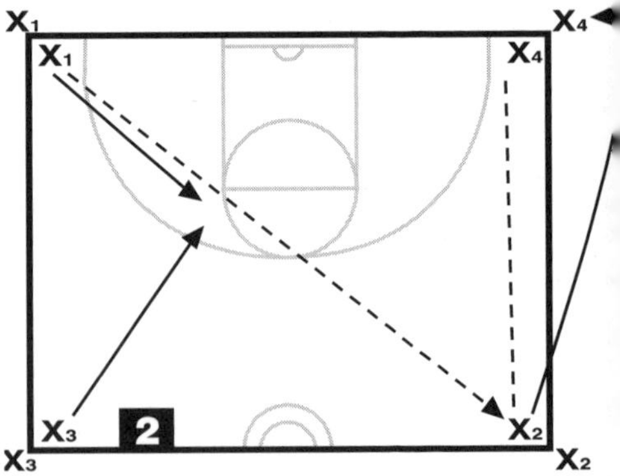

Use the same progression of passes as in the previous drill. X2 does not assume the wing and instead moves to the end of X4's line. X1 makes contact with X3 by cutting off the passing

lane. X1 tries to deny the pass from X4. X3 must move to receive the pass.

If X3 receives the ball, X1 overplays, attempting to draw an offensive foul or have X3 pick up the dribble on the baseline approximately halfway between the basket and the corner. X3's goal is to score. Both players use any means necessary to attain their goals.

TREASURE BALL (DIAGRAM 3)

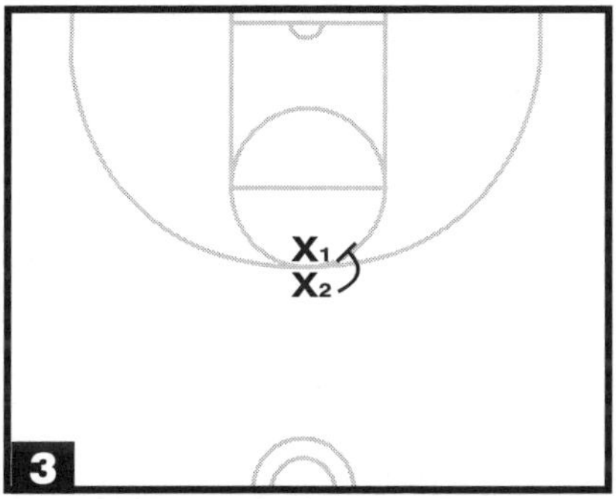

A basketball is placed in the middle of the free throw court circle. X2 stands just outside the circle facing X1. On the coach's signal, X1 cross steps or drops to seal X2 (box cut). X1 tries to maintain this position for 8 seconds, preventing X2 from touching the ball. Both use any means possible.

REBOUND MELEE (DIAGRAM 4)

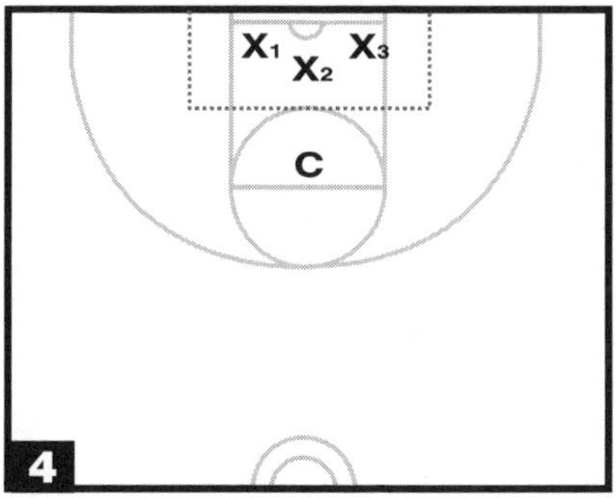

Use three players of approximately the same height. The coach starts out with the ball just under the foul line. The players' area is 1 foot outside the paint on both sides of the baseline and 6 feet from the basket. The coach shoots the ball to start the game.

Players try to score by any means possible within their designated area. Made baskets are considered rebounds.

The first player to score 5 baskets is the winner. If the ball goes out of the designated area, it's passed back to the coach, who quickly shoots to keep the game's continuity.

REBOUND GAME (DIAGRAM 5)

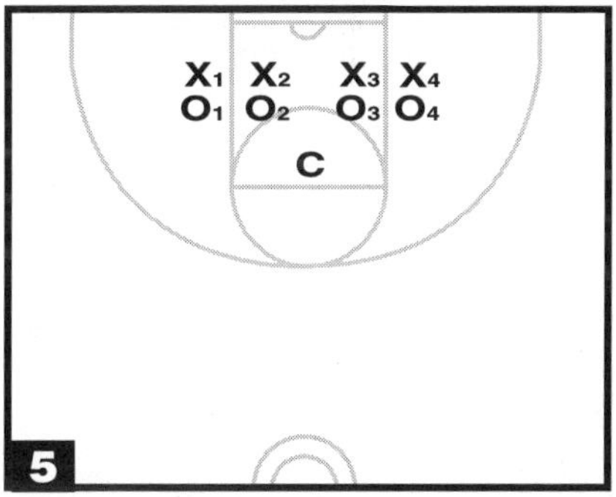

The coach has the ball above the foul line. Four offensive players face the basket in a lineup, directly facing a corresponding defensive player. When the coach shoots the ball the defense yells "shot," boxes their opponents and rebounds the ball.

If the offense secures the rebound, the entire defensive team runs a half-court suicide and immediately gets back to their defensive positions for the next rebound. Players change roles after 5 rebounds.

NO INBOUNDS DRILL (DIAGRAM 6)

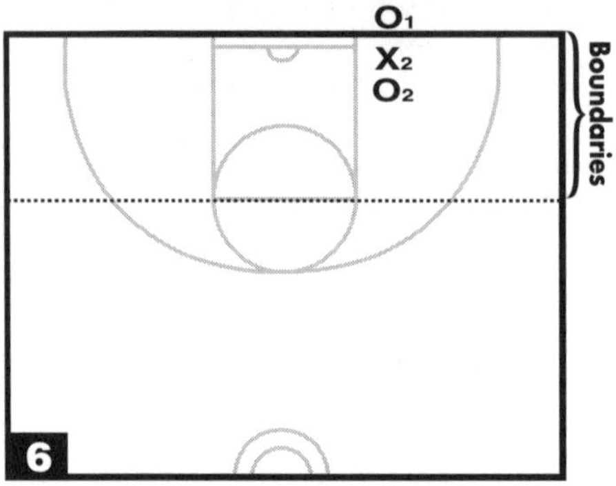

O1 tries to inbound the ball to O2. X2 faces the guards and tries to maintain a position between the ball and O2 in any way possible. If O2 receives an inbound pass they try to score. O2 is restricted in an area from the baseline to the foul line extended. X2 prevents O2 from scoring in any way possible. Rotate as follows: O1, X2, O2, O1.

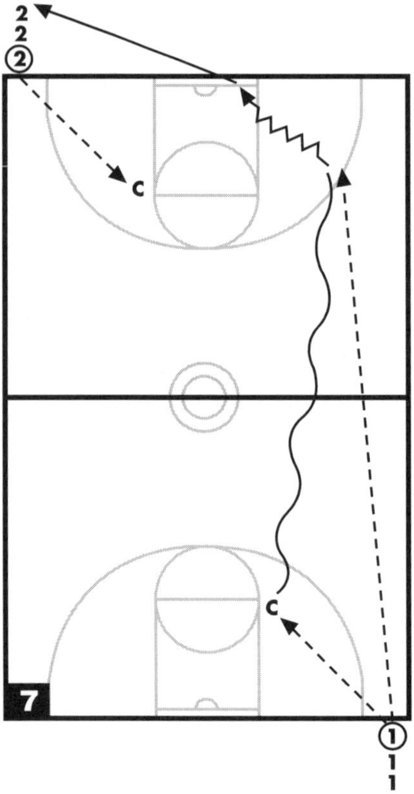

BALL DIVE (DIAGRAM 7)

Each player has a ball and lines up at opposite baseline corners. Two coaches line up diagonally at opposite elbows. Players toss the ball to the coach and take off (release) down court.

Coach rolls the ball down court ahead of the player as a challenge to the player to secure the ball before it goes out of bounds. If the player gets to the ball they attack the basket for a layup, rebound and go to the next line. If the ball goes out of bounds, the player sprints around the court boundary lines.

SCREEN AND ROLL DRILL

This is a 3-on-3 half court game with the following rules:

A. The passer must always screen either the ball or weak side.

B. Every screen must be made with tough and explicit contact.

C. Three points are awarded when the screener scores.

D. Two points are awarded when the cutter scores off the screen.

E. One point is scored when a basket does not involve the screen. There are no fouls in the game.

–Tom Cappello,
Head Men's Coach,
Ansonia High School,
Ansonia, Conn.

Rebounding, Close-Out And Contest The Shooter

THIS DRILL involves three very important aspects of the game:

1. Rebounding.
2. Closeout.
3. Contested shot.

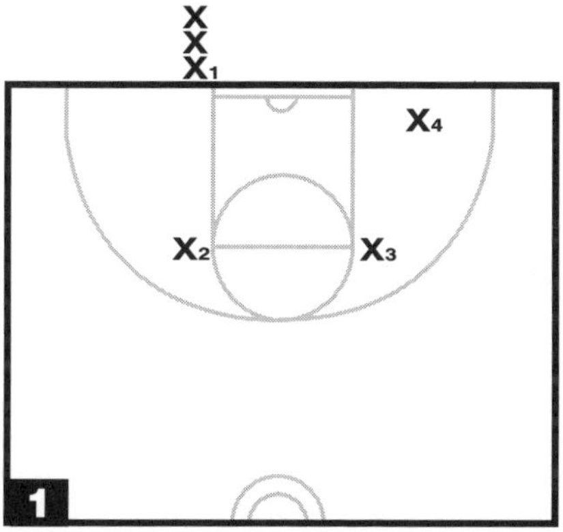

DIAGRAM 1: Players line up under the basket with a player at both elbows and a third player or "shooter" located 2 feet off the low block.

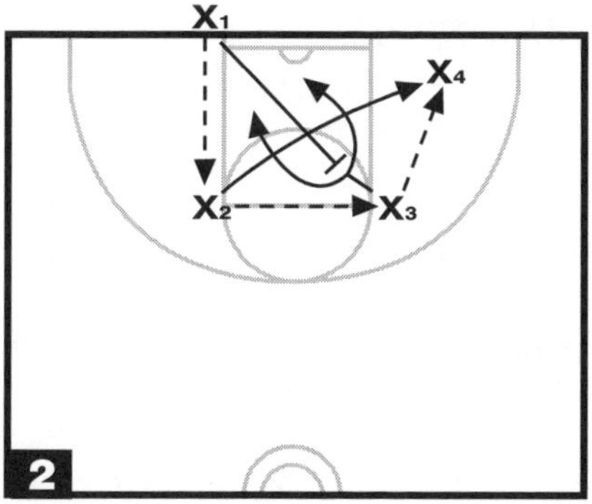

DIAGRAM 2: Player 1 passes to player 2. As soon as player 1 makes the pass to player 2, they go to closeout player 3.

Player 2 passes to player 3. Player 2 then goes to contest player 4.

Player 3, after receiving a pass from player 2, passes to player 4 for the shot.

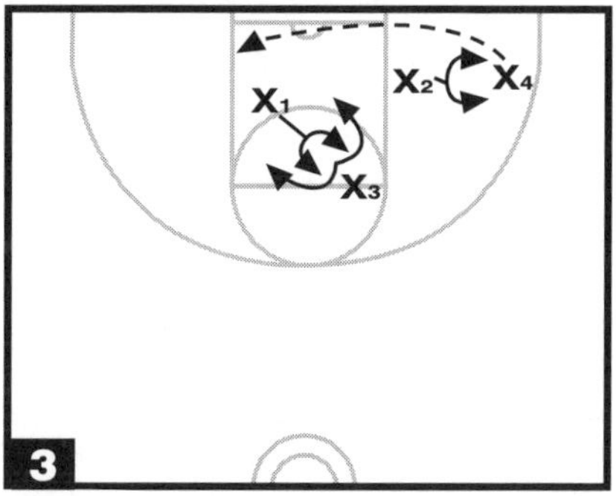

DIAGRAM 3: Player 2 will close-out under control, call for the ball or shot with hands up, then turn and seal.

Player 1 is closing out to box out player 3.

Player 3 can work on gaining position for the offensive rebound.

Rotation:

X1 goes to X2.

X2 goes to X3.

X3 goes to X4.

X4 (shooter) goes to the back of the line.

–George Singleton,
Head Boys' Coach,
Hillcrest High School,
Simpsonville, S.C.

DEFENSIVE FOOTWORK, AGILITY DRILLS

FUNDAMENTAL COMPONENTS...

BUILDING STANCE

Feet: Wide as possible in a heel and toe position, Have your players keep feet spread rather than in a sliding position.

Body, Knees: Chest out, head up, knees parallel to the ground.

Hands: Elbows never past knees, inside hand down in position to hit up on the ball, trail hand up and out looking to be in the passing lane.

Power Foot: This is the foot that's opposite the direction in which the player is moving. Always keep relationship constant as player pushes off power foot and steps with opposite foot.

Change Direction: Very important for player to stay down on change, remaining low while keeping heel and toe relationship and exploding with hands. Change directions.

SLIDE, RUN

Concept: When beat, show player how to pick a spot ahead of the ball.

Technique: Turn shoulders into "sprinters stance." Stay low on run, get angle and lock back in.

CLOSEOUT

Stance: Ball and man, low, wide, cheat, step toward offensive player, cross over step, close out low, head/hands back, be in position that offensive player has to go through chest of defender. Do not close to open stance.

DRILL PROGRESSION...

WALK IT OUT, STANCE

Feet are wide and staggered (heel/toe). Hand on the side of the front is low and digging on the dribble. Hand is on the side of the back, foot is up and out wide trying to get a deflection.

SWITCH, CHANGE DIRECTION

Feet switch positions and the hands explode through the body. Slide twice in the direction of the switch.

1 STEP, 2 STEP, 3 STEP

Start with four lines on the baseline. Players face baseline and slide to half court. Build from one step to three.

SLIDE RUN SLIDE

Use four lines. Slide. Get beat. Turn shoulders, touch the floor, run to get ahead and lock back in a stance and slide.

2-MAN MIRROR

Players get a partner. Same four lines. Both are in a defensive stance and tight into each other's body. One player acts as the offensive player, shouting commands as they perform them and their partner must react and mirror them.

WING DENIAL

Use two lines on the baseline. First two players step out to the block. Put someone on each wing and at the point. Players must see the ball. Slide out and deny the wing three times quickly. Add back door and dribble help.

CLOSEOUTS AND WING CLOSEOUTS

Use four lines on the baseline. Players all face the same sideline. Position someone at the head of each line, even with the top of the key. Players get in a stance/help position.

Coach calls cheat and they inch toward the shooter before closing and sprinting to the shooter.

Have your players stay low to the ground, chop step as they get close and get into a stance. Hands swing up through the body and into the line of vision. Do two lines and close out on each wing. Close out to denial in good denial stance, palm to ball;, ear in chest, measuring distance between the ball and man.

HELP, CLOSE, DENY-HELP

Players start in a group facing the coach. They get in a help position. They cheat, close, jump off, deny and sprint back to a help position. They all go at once and repeat in both directions.

REACT TO THE COACH, LINE MIRROR

Players start in a group facing the coach. They get in a help position. They cheat, then close, then jump off and deny, then sprint back to a help position. They all go at once and repeat in both directions.

SLIP SCREEN

A player on each wing denies an offensive player trying to free up. Another player down screens and back screens on the wings and the defender slips the screen with a swim-type move.

CHASE, EXTEND

Bump and get off to help on the down screen. Have the stand-up man accepting a screen. On screen down, the man defending the screen "extends," keeping contact with the screener. Player defending the player and taking the screen gets on the hip and chases man off the screen.

DENY AND HELP SUPPORT

The setup is for the two-guard front unguarded with two offensive wing players and two defenders. The ball is passed guard-to-guard. Players must react and deny to help as the ball is moved. Add a weak side flash as the ball is reversed.

COMBINATION

Players form a line at a corner of the court. They step up the sideline and at half court turn and deny. At the other sideline go slide, run, slide; on the baseline go two steps. Do the same from the other court. Repeat twice.

–Mike Madagan,
Assistant Coach,
University of South Florida,
Tampa, Fla.

"Nothing can stop the person with the right mental attitude from achieving their goal. Nothing on earth can help the person with the wrong mental attitude."

FOOTWORK DRILLS

LINE MIRROR (#1)

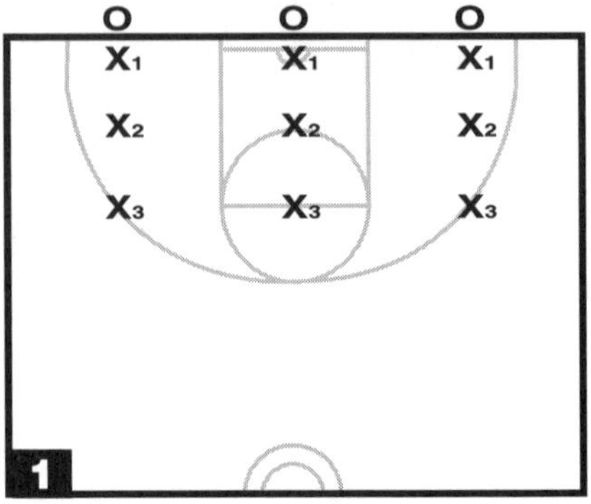

X1 is into O, tracing the ball, applying good hand pressure with hands above the ball. X2 and X3 also stimulate guarding O. O will drive the ball side-to-side up the floor. X must react. Drill ends with a pass and jump to deny, or a shot and block out.

DENY SUPPORT (#2,3,4)

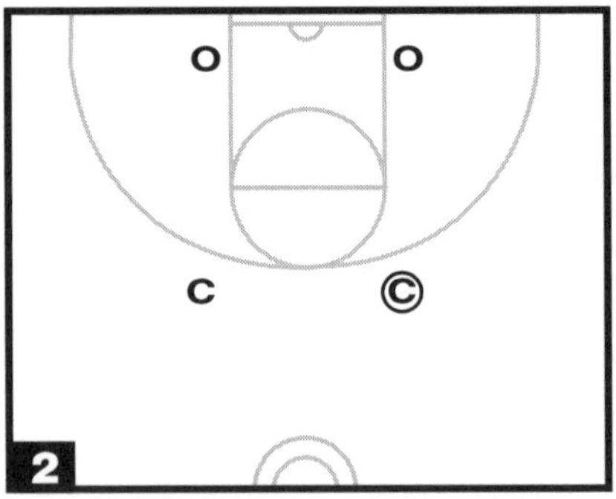

X1 is in deny position one pass away, measuring distance in relation to the ball. X2 is in the help position, two passes away in a closed stance, talking off the ball. X1 denies lead, not allowing O to get into their body while staying up the line.

X2 is ready to prevent flash and help on the drive. Ball is reversed and the drill is repeated on the other side.

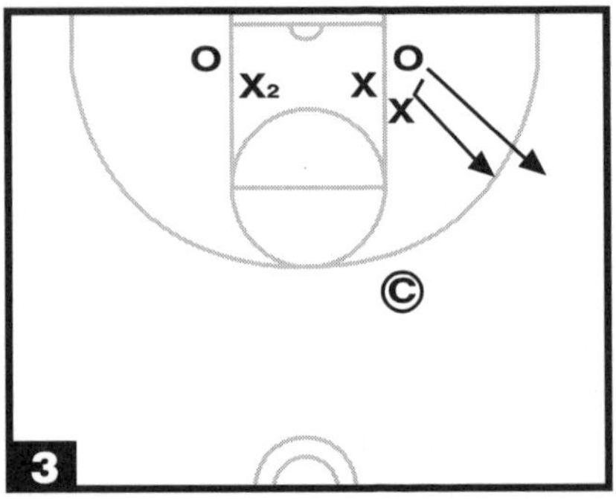

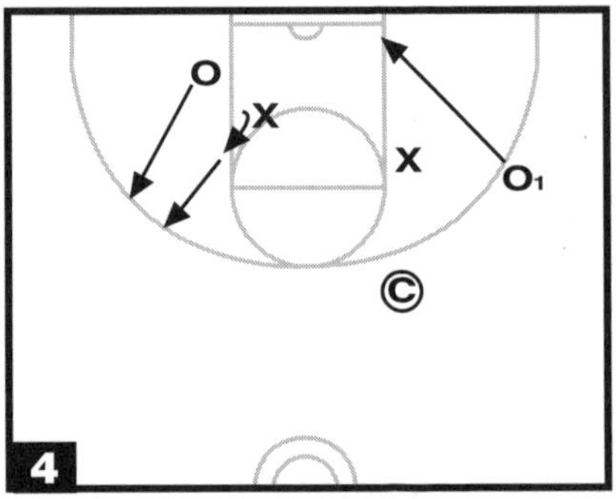

LINE CLOSEOUT (#5,6)

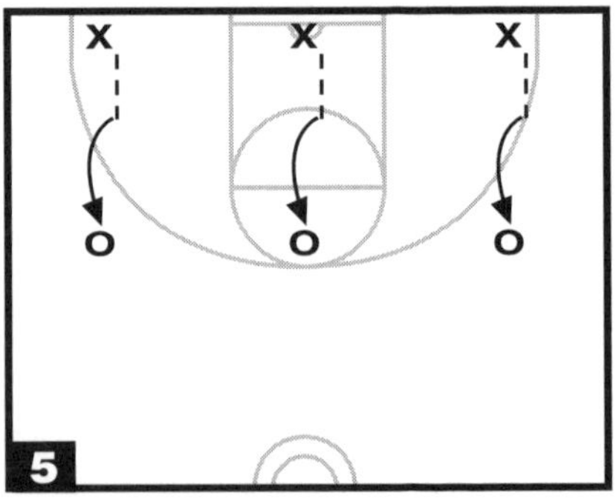

X is in an off-the-ball stance, pointing to man and ball. On command, players cheat to man and closeout on O. Keep weight back and have your players make the offense go through your chest.

X pressures O and O zig-zags back

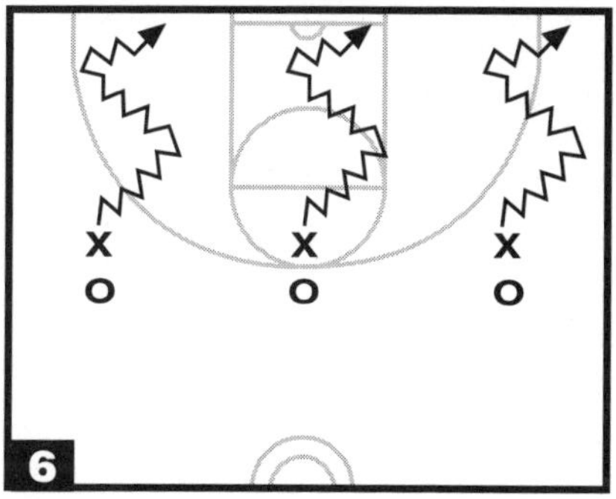

to the baseline. X uses footwork to keep the ball out in front.

WING CLOSEOUT (#7)

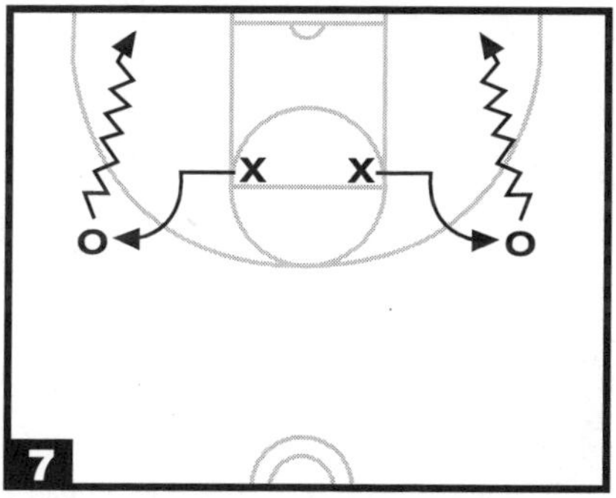

X is in a help position as the coach raises hand, X cheats toward O and then closes. O drives the ball and X forces to baseline checkpoint.

CHECK POINT DRIVING LINE (#8)

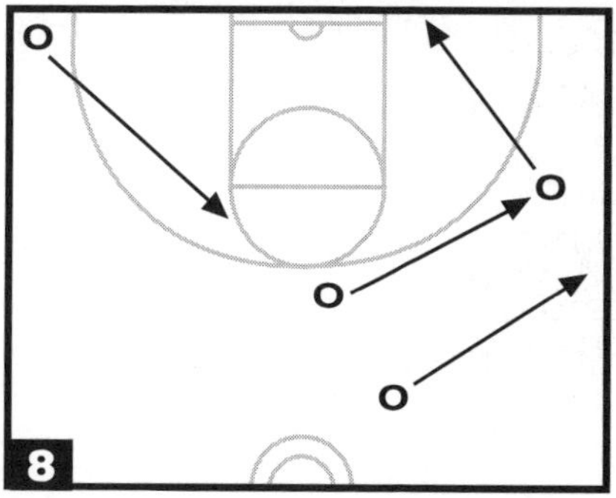

Pressure stance. Defend an imaginary offensive player, forcing driving angle to an appropriate check point. It ends on a dead ball, pass and jump.

ALL IN ONE

PRESSURE, TRACE, SLIDE (#9)

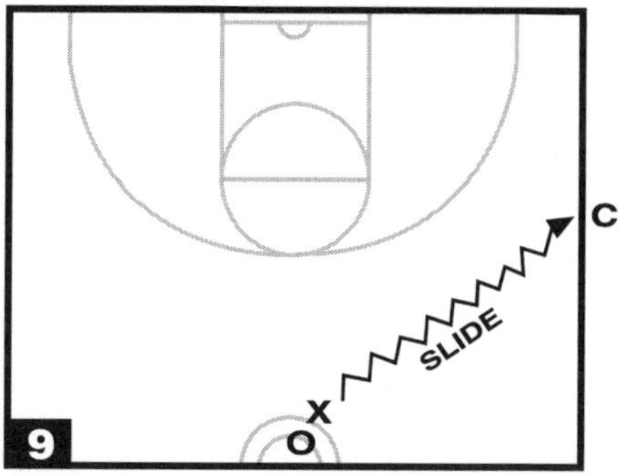

Drill begins with X up and into O, tracing the ball. X then slides to C.

DEAD-JUMP TO THE BALL, BLUFF (#10)

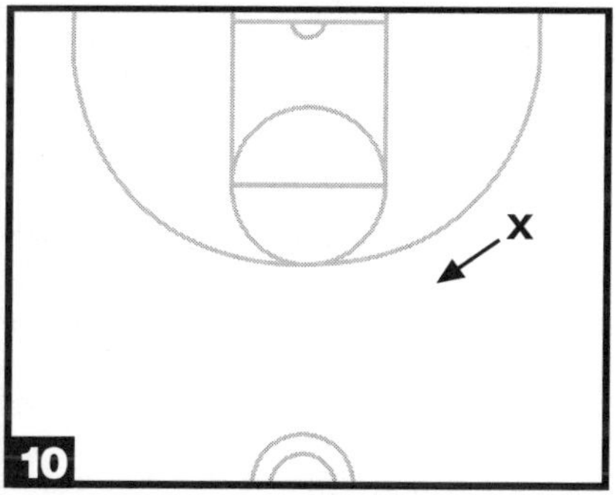

X gets to dead stance, jumps to the ball and bluffs in the gap to deter penetration.

CHEAT, SPRINT TO HELP, CLOSE (#11)

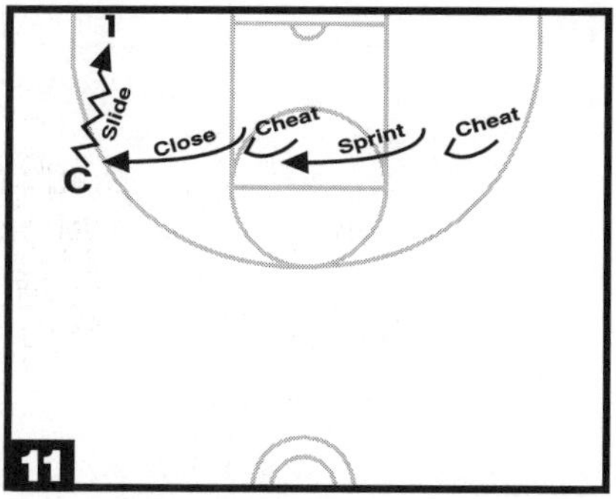

X stays in a stance and cheats toward the lane. X then cross over steps and sprints to help, gets floor position in relation to the coach. Then X cheats toward other coach and closes hard.

DEAD-JUMP, BLUFF, SPRINT TO HELP (#12)

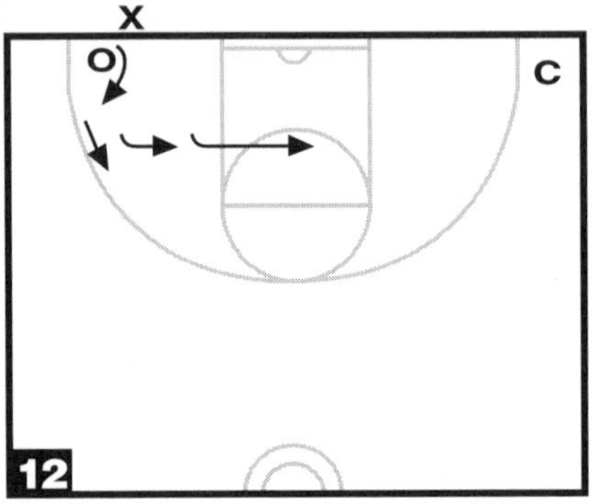

X now gets to a dead stance, jumps off to deny and actively bluffs in the gap, then sprints to help, cheat, close and block out.

1-ON-1 BLOCK OUT (#13)

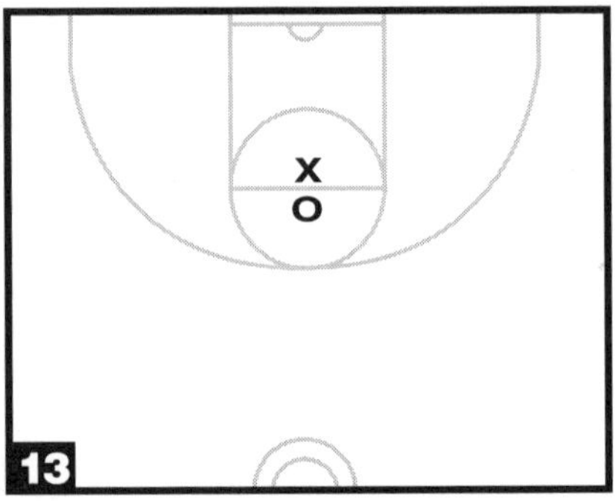

O runs a straight line to the rim. X jams them head on, then reverse pivots while staying low and spreading out to hold O off. Elbows are out and hands are high.

2-ON-2 BLOCK OUT (#14)

X1 and X2 get position in relation to the ball and their men. On the shot, O gets to rim and X must jam and block out.

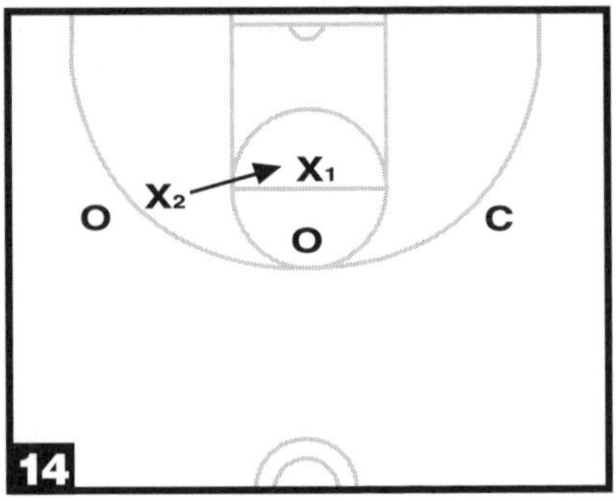

3-ON-3 BLOCK OUT(#15)

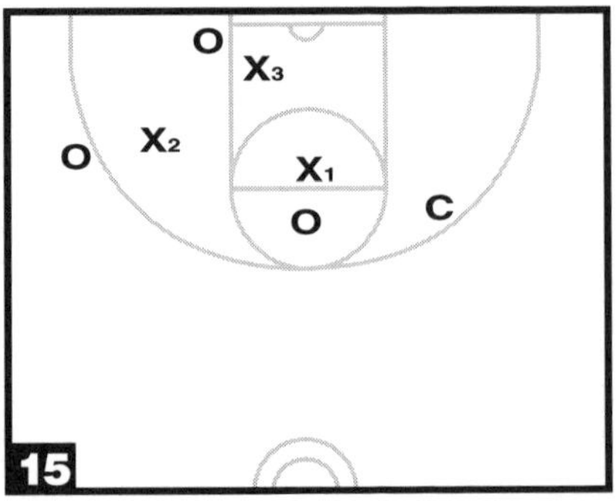

Same as above. Defenders must get proper floor position. Play continues until defense gets a rebound. (Movement away from the ball and by the ball will help stimulate game-like conditions).

5-ON-5 TRANSITION DEFENSE (#16)

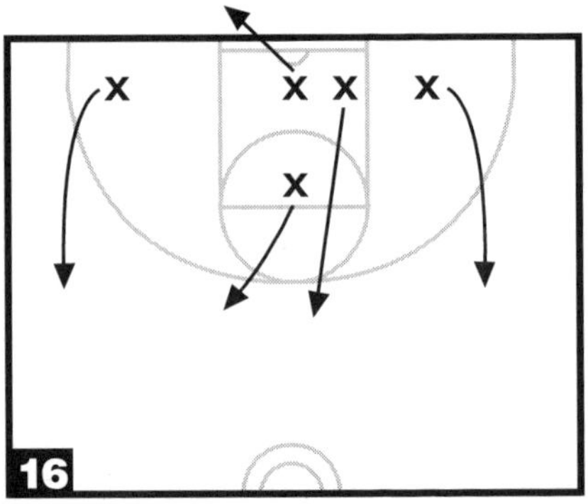

This begins with a block out while pushing the ball and running the break.

Keep the wings wide and point in mid-point. 4-man in the middle of the floor, 5 gap. X1 will play ball up the floor. X5 will wait on offensive end. O1 defends ball up the floor.

On a made basket, X5 turns, O4 now pushes ball. O5 supports. O2, O3 and O4 run the floor and touch man, then get off to help and bluff and retreat while the post player goes up the line. O1 contains the ball up the floor with support from the 5 man.

5-ON-5 DEFENSIVE TRANSITION (#17)

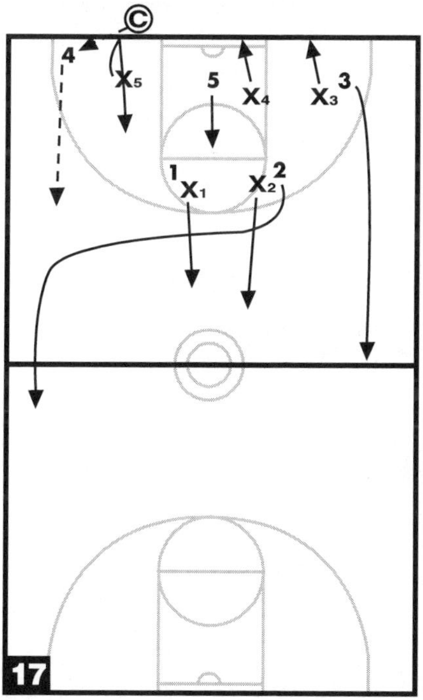

The coach passes to 3, 4 or 5. The two defenders of the players that didn't catch the ball must touch the baseline and then recover. All others recover back immediately. Communication among players is a must.

2-ON-2 FRENZY BUILD UP (#18)

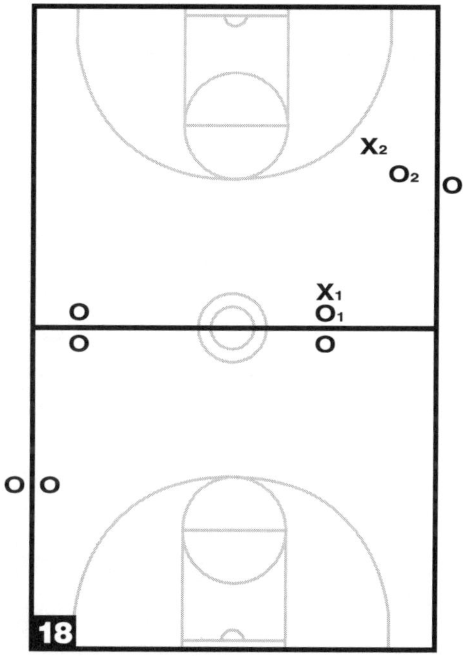

Stay on the half court. O1 tries to drive or enter to O2. O2 tries to create a lead. X1 and X2 play solid defense fundamentals. On rebounding the ball, X2 hand-over-head passes to next player at half court. Offense sprints closest to defensive position.

With a 3-on-3 situation, it is the same as above, but now add a post player. On basket or stop, X outlets the ball to half court. Offense now sprints to close and defends the next possession.

"The race is not always won by the fastest runner, but sometimes by those who just keep on running."

4-ON-4 FRENZY DRILL (#19)

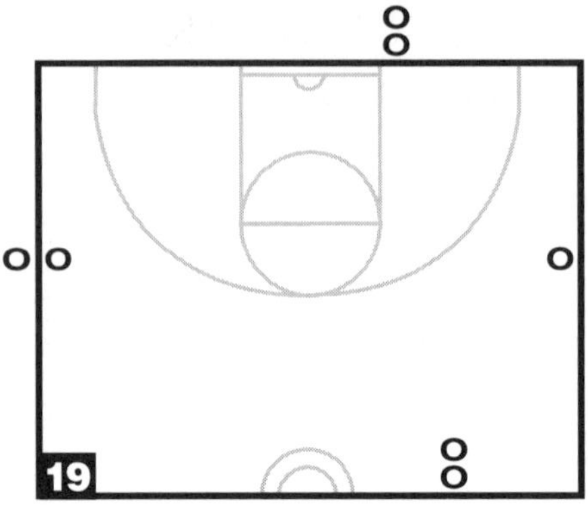

Same as with # 18, but add a second wing.

4-ON-6 FRENZY DRILL (#20)

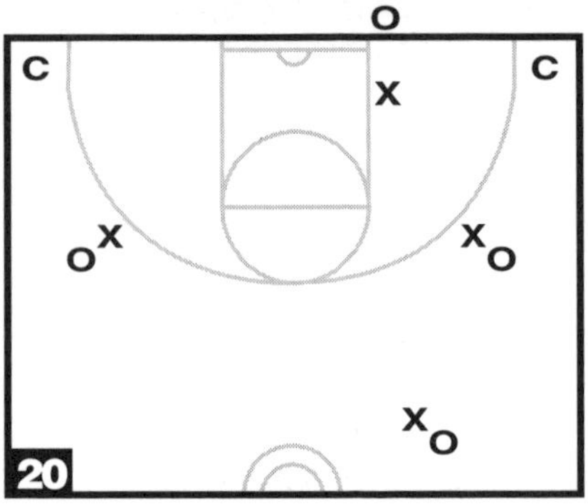

Same as with #19, but add coaches or managers in the corners for dribble penetration and as passers.

By Mike Madagan,
University of South Florida,
Tampa, Fla.

THREE-WAY "ZIG-ZAG" DRILL

- ✘ Emphasize guarding dribbler for more than two or three dribblers in one direction.
- ✘ Player goes to center of court instead of the lane.
- ✘ Allow offense more freedom.
- ✘ Emphasize foot movement (outside foot back in each direction).

3 Ways

1. Hands behind back.
2. Hands on shirt.
3. Using hands.

–Mack McCarthy,
Head Men's Basketball Coach,
Virginia Commonwealth,
Richmond, Va.

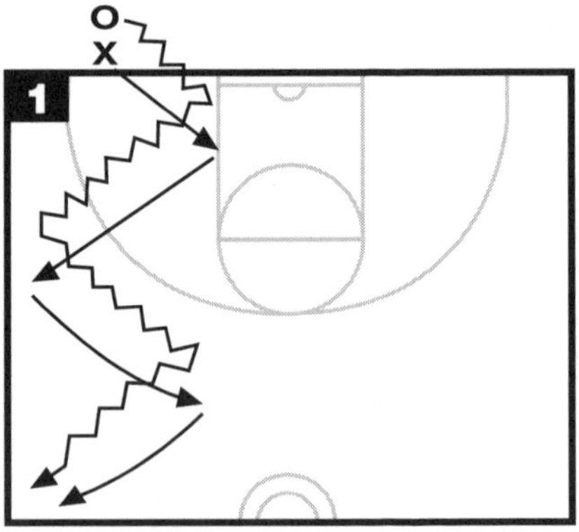

1-ON-1 DEFENSIVE TRANSITION DRILL

1-ON-1

Guard each other.

On your verbal command of "change," the offense throws the ball to the defense and the players switch roles. (O becomes D, D becomes O).

–Mack McCarthy,
Head Basketball Coach,
Virginia Commonwealth,
Richmond, Va.

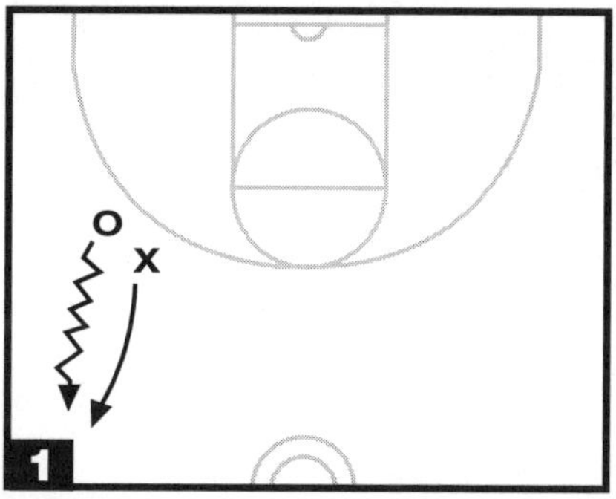

MAN-TO-MAN DEFENSIVE DRILLS

"REBOUNDING SHELL" (#1)

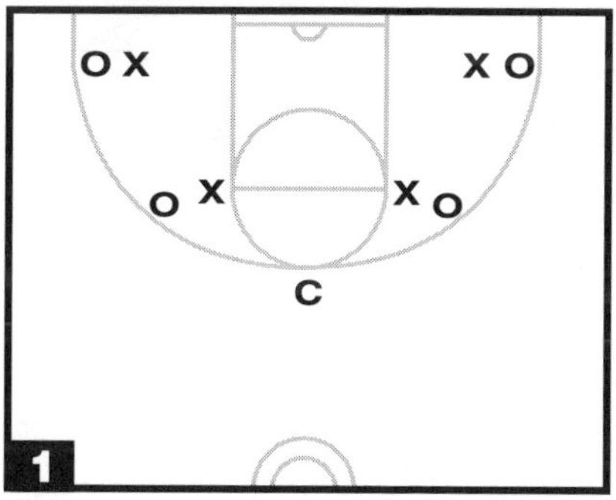

1. Emphasize contact and release to the ball.
2. 2 points for every rebound.

"BLOOD AND GUTS" (#2)

1. 1-on-1 rebounding.
2. 1-on-2 rebounding.
3. Player can start underneath or from the free-throw line. Typically played until three made baskets.

"ROLL BALL" (#3)

1. Player blocks to wing and defends or lane to point and defends.
2. Defense rolls the ball to offense.
3. Emphasis is on correct defensive technique or attacking offensive man and breaking down in time to stop the drive.

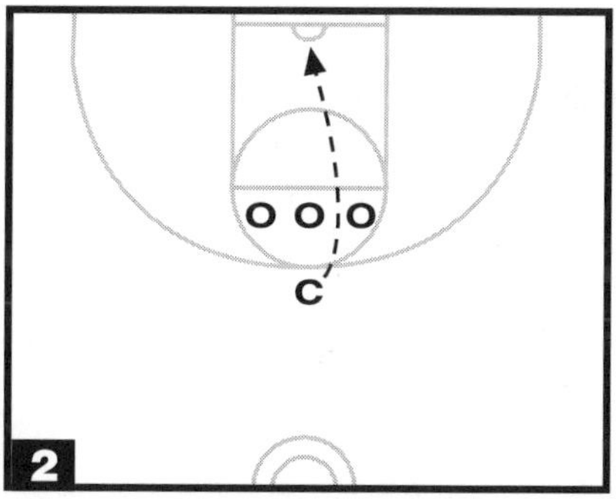

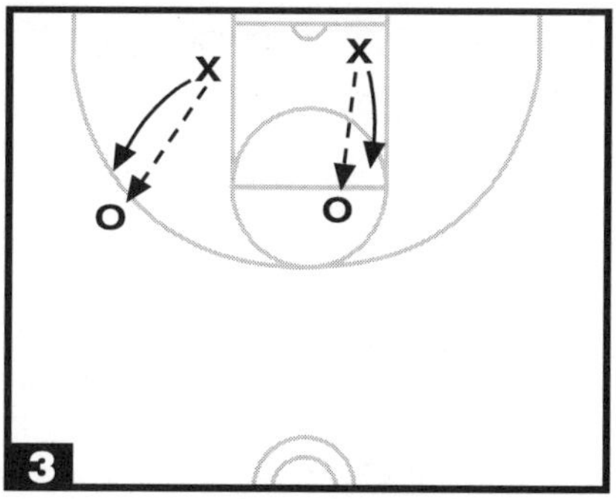

Mack McCarthy,
Virginia Commonwealth,
Richmond, Va.

Chapter 5

GAME SITUATIONS

5-MAN "CONTINUOUS" FAST BREAK

REASONS FOR RUNNING "CONTINUOUS" BREAK

1. Excellent for shooting layups at full speed.

2. Excellent for passing as chest, bounce and baseball passes are required.

3. Excellent for conditioning.

RULES AND ROTATION OF PLAYERS

1. Shooter goes back to the half court line on the same side they shot from.

2. Rebounder goes to half court line on the side they pass the ball to.

3. The player that passes to the shooter pivots in the corner, sprints down side-line and shoots at opposite basket.

4. The shooter should always use the backboard.

5. The players returning to half court should run back and touch the line with their foot.

6. No fumbled passes.

7. The ball should touch the floor only when bounced to the shooter.

This is diagrammed for a right-hand layup. It can be run on either side. Just start 3 players on shooting side with 2 players on opposite side.

DIAGRAM 1: The drill starts with an alignment of three players on the right side and two players on left side. 1 has the ball, 2 breaks to the free-throw line and receives a chest pass from 1. 1 will

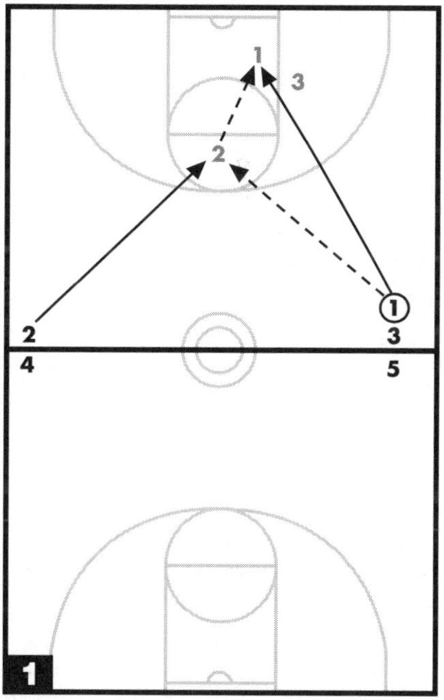

receive bounce pass from 2 and shoot a layup. 3 rebounds while not letting the ball hit the floor.

DIAGRAM 2: After a bounce pass, 2 pivots in the corner, sprints down the sideline behind 4 and shoots a layup at the opposite basket. 3 makes a baseball pass to 4 and goes to that side while 1 returns to the side they shot from.

DIAGRAM 3: After receiving a pass from 3, 4 throws a chest pass to 5, who throws bounce pass to 2, who shoots a layup.

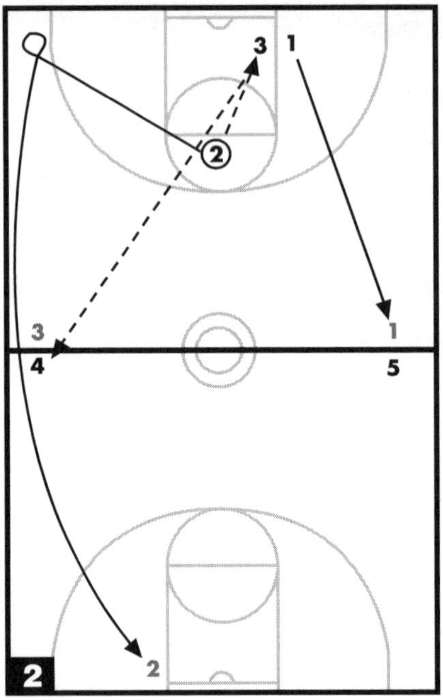

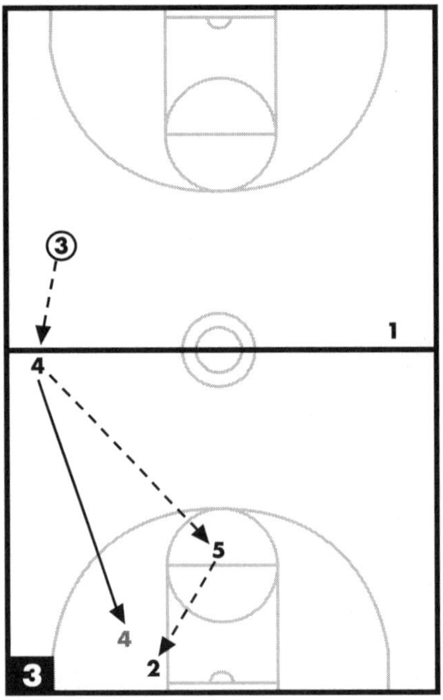

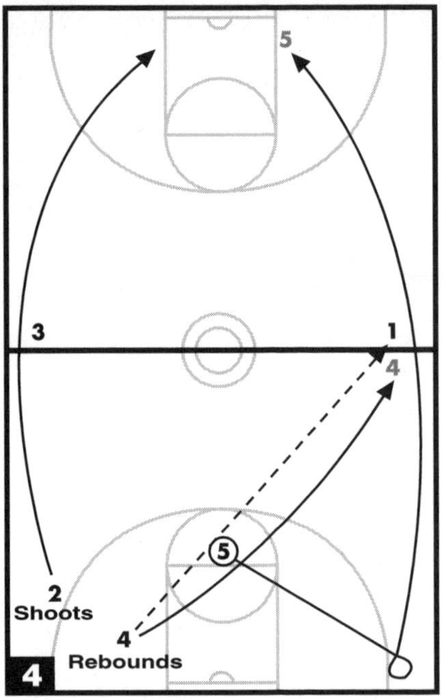

DIAGRAM 4: After bounce passing to 2, 5 pivots in the corner, sprints down the sideline behind 1 and becomes the next shooter. 4 rebounds, throws a baseball pass to 1 and goes to the side that he passed to. 2 then returns to the side that he shot from.

CONTINUITY CONTINUES

We've run this break at the start of practice for a warm-up drill and at the end of practice for conditioning. Sometimes we give players 2 minutes to make a certain number of shots. Sometimes we give players a certain number to make in a row.

—Jerry White,
Hampton High School,
Hampton, Tenn.

Layup Drills

OUTLET PASS LAYUP DRILL

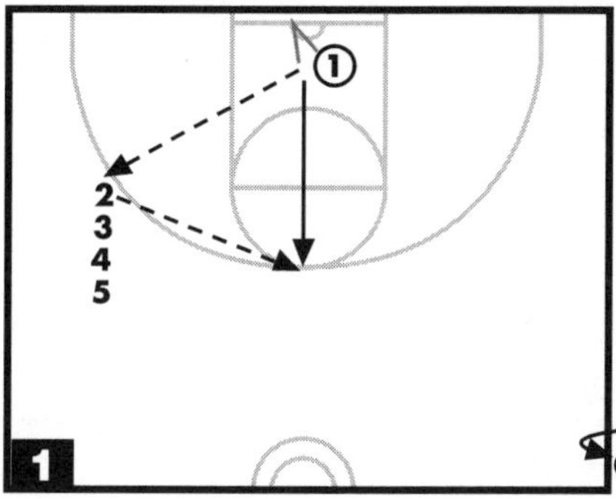

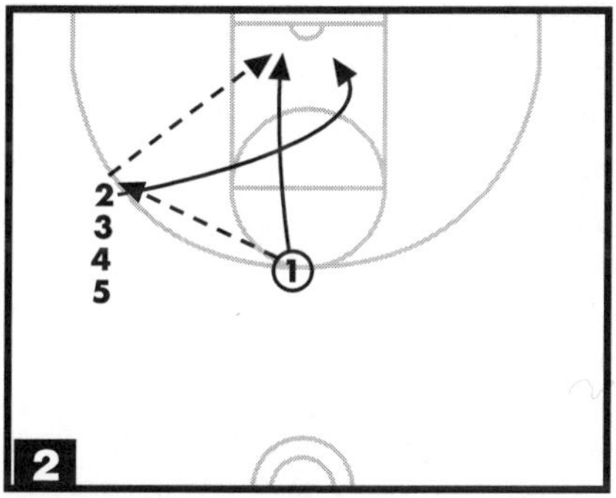

FIGURES 1 AND 2: Players line up behind one another on the wing. 1 starts the drill by tossing the ball on the backboard and rebounding that toss. Following that, they turn to the outside and outlet the ball to 2.

Upon outletting the ball, they sprint to the top of the key to receive a return pass from 2. They then pass the ball back to 2 and sprint to the basket. 2 passes the ball back to 1 and follows their pass to rebound the made or missed shot by 1. 2 continues the drill and 1 goes to the end of the line. Each player should go three to five times on each side.

HALF-COURT PASSING LAYUP DRILL OR WARM-UP DRILL

This is a warm-up drill for use with two basketballs. Use this for a change of pace layup drill or as a warm-up drill. It is used to improve passing skills, quickness and timing. Points of emphasis:

1. Sharp passes.

2. Proper pivot on the outlet pass.

3. Making hard cuts to the basket.

HALF-COURT PASSING LAYUP DRILL

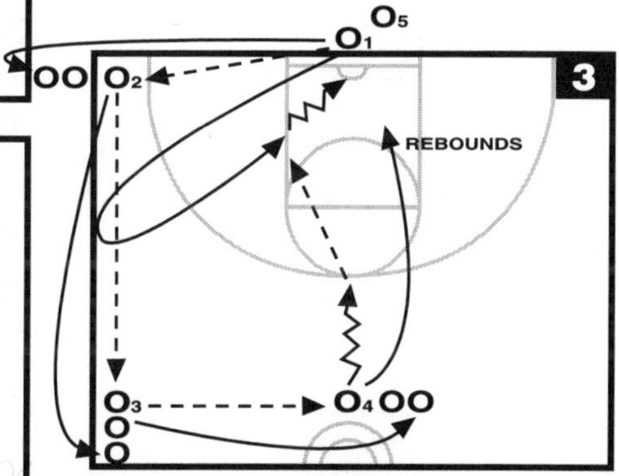

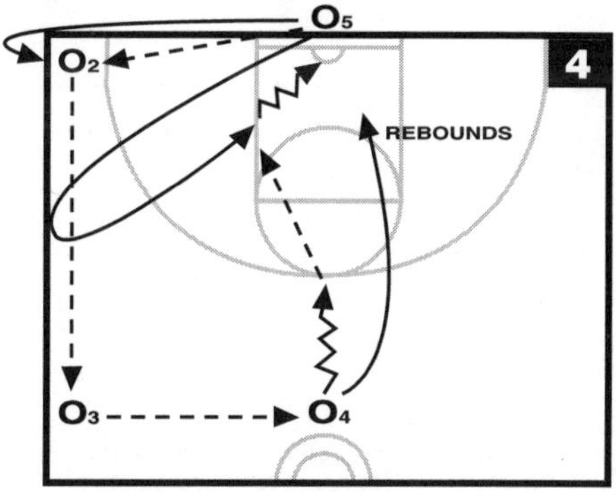

FIGURES 3 AND 4: Divide your players into four lines as diagrammed. Two players begin the drill with basketballs under the basket. 1 begins by passing the ball to 2. 2 passes the ball to 3. 3 then passes to 4. 4 takes two dribbles and will pass the ball to 1, who sprinted to the sideline after they passed the ball to 2 and returned for a

layup. 4 will rebound and continue the drill.

After 1 passes the ball to 2 and 2 passes to 3, then 6 begins with a pass to line 2 so that two basketballs are used in this drill.

The players follow their passes so they are rotating in a counterclockwise fashion. 1 goes to line 2, 2 goes to line 3, 3 goes to 4 and the 1 player will go to line 2 after they take the layup.

We use a couple of excellent one-on-one drills to help players use their moves and propel them to a higher level of play. We want our players to be offensive threats so they can take the ball to the basket if the defensive player is beat.

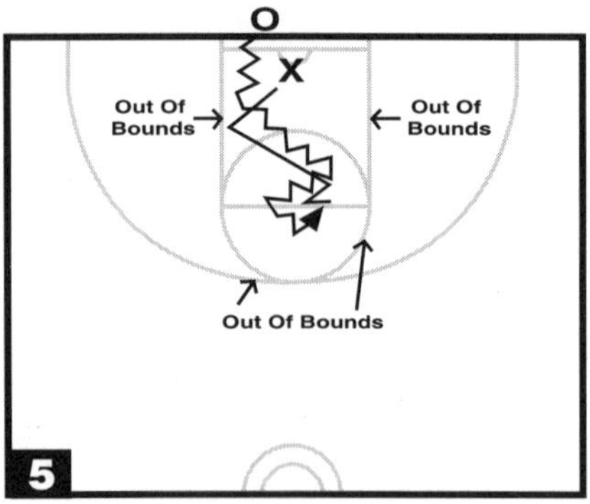

FIGURE 5: Player starts underneath the basket with a ball. After dribbling up the lane and touching the free-throw line with their foot, they attack the basket. The lane is in play while outside the lane is a turnover.

When the player shoots a basket inside the key and foul line, it's worth 2 points. Any other made shot is 1 point. The game is played to a score of 11 points.

The players get good conditioning and will have lots of pressure getting the ball back out as they try and take the ball to the basket while blocking out.

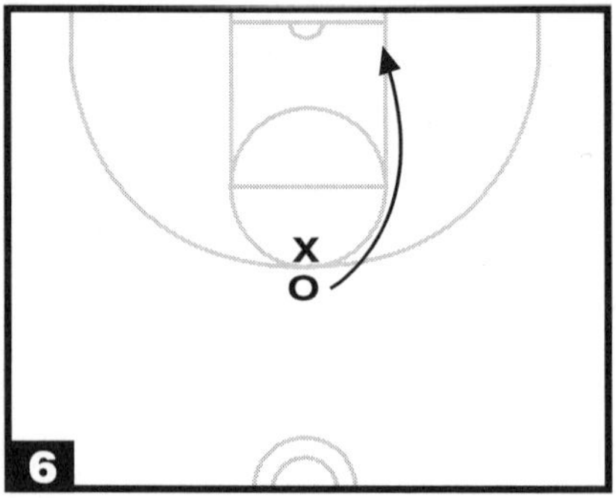

FIGURE 6: This is another one-on-one drill to defend on the individual defensive play. Players begin at the top of the key. They try taking the ball to the basket, with some rules in place:

1. Games go up to 11 points.

2. A basket made with only one dribble is worth 2 points.

3. A basket made without dribbling is worth 3 points.

4. A basket made using two dribbles is worth 1 point.

5. If the offensive player scores, they retain the basketball.

These drills will improve your player's offensive skills and individual defensive play.

—Bill Kunze,
Assistant Coach,
Duluth East High School,
Duluth, Minn.

"Continuous effort, not strength or intelligence, is the key to unlocking our potential."
— Liane Corder

Bulldog Transition Series

OUR COACHING STAFF IS committed to a transition style of basketball. In developing and refining our style of play, we've studied the concepts and drills of as many top-notch transition programs as possible.

The Bulldog transition series is a hybrid of a few drills we really liked and incorporated into our daily practice structure.

SCHEDULING CONCERNS

Spend the first 15 minutes of each pre-season practice, along with the first 10 minutes of your regular season practices, running this series. Doing so accomplishes two major objectives:

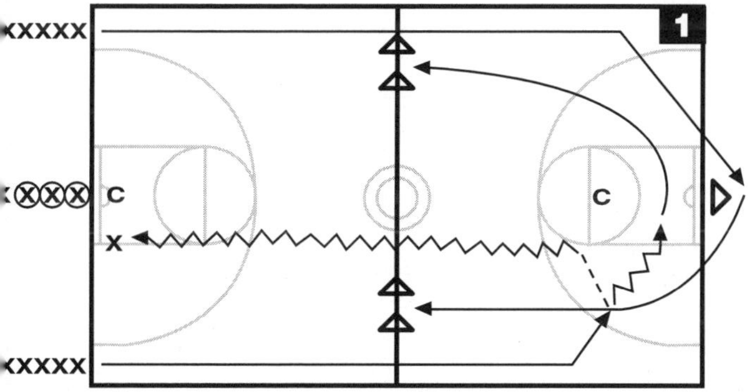

1. It develops a love for, and not just a tolerance of, running the floor.

2. It develops all the skills necessary for becoming a good transition player.

The series is broken into two parts consisting of layups and jump shooting and begins with your squad members lined up in three equal lines on the baseline.

Place three basketballs on the middle line. Four corners (pylons) are placed at half court to create outside running lanes on the way down and inside lanes on the way back. Another cone is placed on the baseline in the middle of the floor at the other end. Use a traditional line rotation of middle to right, left to middle. Run the series an equal amount of time to both sides of the floor.

It's important to emphasize that the middle line of players should always dribble the ball to the side of the right or left foul lane line. This keeps the ball handlers from running into each other. Put a coach at the other elbow area to insure the passer comes to a jump stop. Put another coach under the basket to insure that players shoot a power layup on the way back.

The series starts with the dribbler pushing the ball to the elbow at the other end of the floor. The two lane runners sprint in

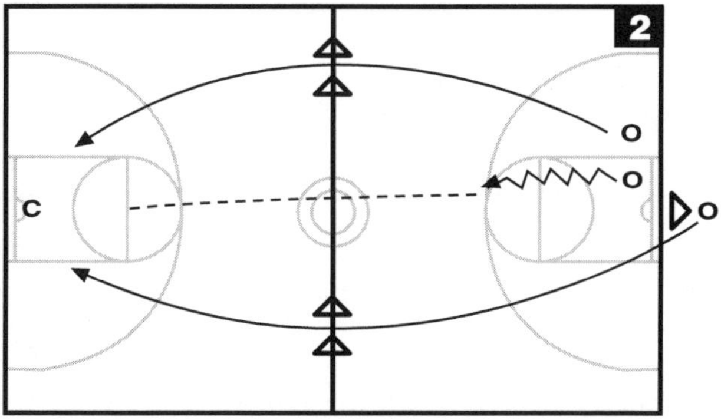

the outside lanes and make 45-degree cuts to the basket. The dribbler jump stops and makes a bounce pass to the designated side for a layup. They shoot and continue through to the opposite side, filling the inside lane.

The other lane runner goes underneath the cone and sprints back up the other inside lane. They look for a diagonal full-court pass from the dribbler, who gets the ball out of the net or off the board and pushes the dribble back up the opposite side. (A pass is often made in transition basketball).

WORK HARD BOTH WAYS

Have players shoot a power layup on the return trip, making sure the ball

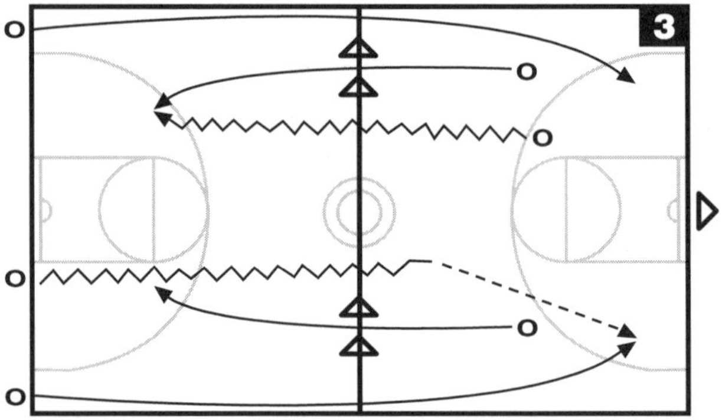

is transferred to the opposite side of the body and away from the defense. The beauty of this series is that at the exact time the dribbler gets the ball at the opposite end, the next group is leaving in the original direction. This keeps six players moving at all times, making the conditioning benefits obvious.

The jump shot series is run exactly the same way with two differences. First, the lane runners come back on the same side of the floor. Second, the dribbler penetrates to the elbow on each end and makes a pitch pass to the corner for the perimeter player to shoot a 3-point shot, or to the post players shooting a 12 to 15 foot bank shot.

The key in keeping the timing of the series going is for the next wave of players not to begin until the dribbler on the other end gets the ball back in their hands.

Running the bulldog transition series in every practice really helps to develop the transition mentality that all up-tempo teams need. You can easily customize this drill to your needs with goals for made or missed layups and jump shots.

—Mike Flynn,
Head Men's Coach,
Holmes High School,
Covington, Ky.

"Failure is only temporary and never permanent, unless you let it be."

"Stinger" Drills To Improve Your Transition Game

ALL COACHES KNOW that players improve their skills through hard work and repetition of drills during practice and not just by a "scrimmage." While these skills may include shooting, ball handling and rebounding, they should not include playing full court games. This type of game should be saved for days when there's a scheduled game.

My philosophy is to never play games in practice. Practices should be reserved for developing a player's individual skills. At best, coaches should only use a variation of game situations. Most coaches also realize their players' patience can only be held for short amounts of time if the drills in practice are considered "boring." Time management and creativity of skill drills become essential for a successful practice.

As a result, my assistant and I have devised a means of combining excitement and skill building into full court drills for our practices. We call these drills "Stingers" (since our mascot is a yellow jacket) and practice them every day.

There are three "Stinger" drills that consume less than 20 minutes of each practice. The drills will ultimately help develop the individual and team passing game, along with court awareness and decision making. It's also an exciting way to end each practice session.

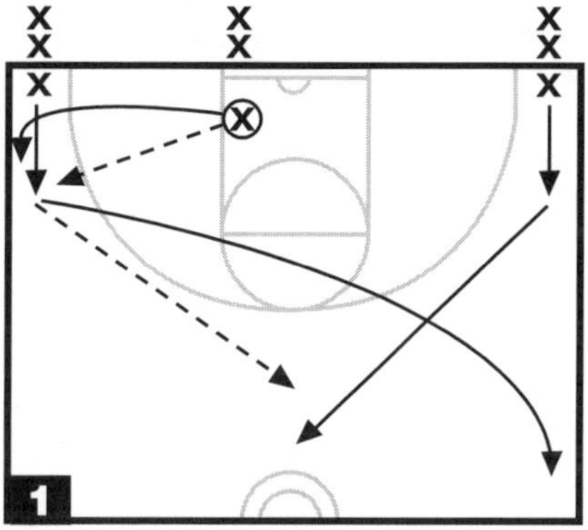

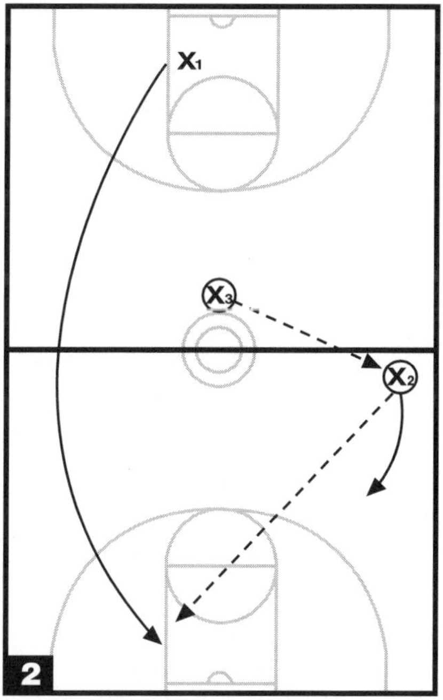

STINGER DRILL #1

The first "Stinger" drill is a basic three-man weave drill that we call "weave." Put 3 minutes on the clock and split the players into groups of three. Each group must successfully complete the drill three times. The drill teaches players to have wide court spacing and make long passes on the run.

The rules are simple: each player runs behind the player to whom they passed the ball, similar to all weave drills. There is a four-pass limit, no one may dribble and the group must end with a layup.

Begin with three lines of players on

the baseline. The players on the sidelines are "wings," while the center line under the basket is for "forwards." Look closely for correct fundamental work in this drill. The man in the middle line starts the drill by throwing the ball off the backboard and jumping to grab it with two hands held over their head.

At the same time, the wings sprint out to the foul line extended and yell "outlet." The player with the ball pivots towards a sideline and fires a pass to the wing. The opposite wing sprints to half court, where they'll receive the next pass. Thus a three-man weave continues down the floor, making sure the rules are followed.

Players will often rush passes, travel, forget to jump stop or not be in position to make a smooth layup. By the third day, the team will have corrected these common mistakes.

Teams will begin to notice a big difference in their fast-breaking ability and overall improvement in quickness during the transition game. To emphasize the fundamentals, penalize teams if there's a mistake by returning them to the front of the line and immediately trying the drill again. This goes for dribbling, turnovers, bad passes or whatever you decide to concentrate on in practice.

STINGER DRILL #2

By the third practice, add the second of the "Stinger" drills. Put six minutes on the clock to complete this drill. This is where players begin to work on the transition game with defenders by using the basic "weave" to start off. The wing who catches the ball at midcourt is now the point guard.

This group will now attack the basket against two pre-chosen defenders, trying to score a basket off both a layup and a jump shot. The two defenders will begin at half court. Once the ball hits the backboard to start the drill, they will run on defense. Don't encourage players to shoot 3-point baskets.

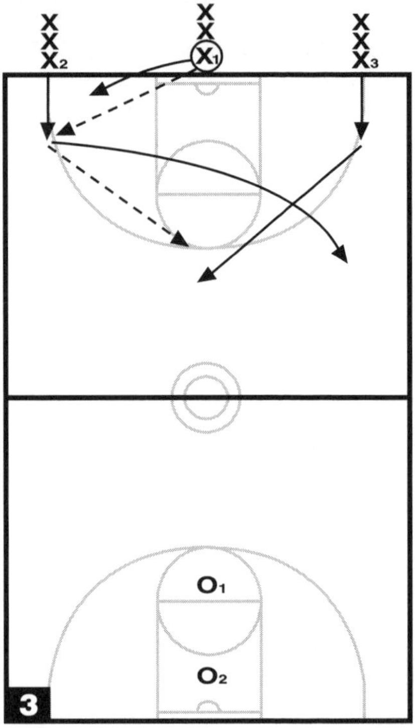

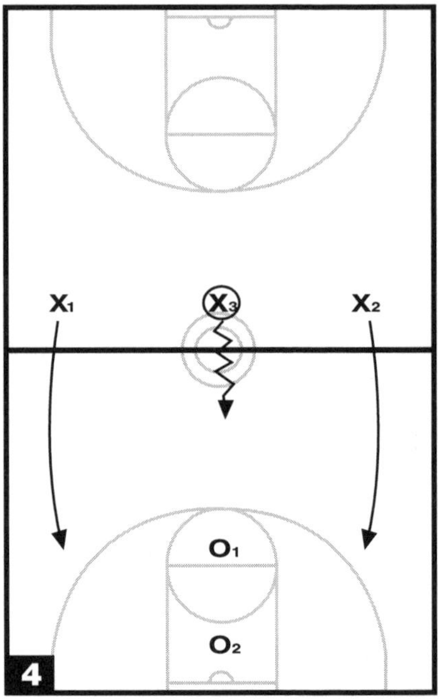

The player on offense who commits a turnover or shoots the ball (make or miss) will sprint to the other end and play defense against the two original defenders, who have now become the offense. Again, we're looking for a layup followed by a jump shot.

It's important not to penalize the entire team for making a mistake. Keep it confined to penalizing individual players only. The player who makes a mistake must do five pushups while the next group is running the drill. Again, penalize players for poor fundamental work.

STINGER #3 SENT DEFENDERS

The final "Stinger" drill is where your assistant coach becomes important. Add this drill to the other three and split the team into two groups, with one on offense and the other on defense.

Score during this drill is kept just like in a real game. Each team gets five minutes to score as many points as possible. The offensive team lines up on the baseline with equal spacing, facing forward with the defense on the sideline at half court with the assistant coach.

The middle man, usually the center, starts the drill like the weave—the two sideline players are the wings while the other two inner players are forwards. The wing players will complete the weave to mid-court while the forwards end the break while attacking the defense at the other end.

When the ball is thrown off the backboard, any number of players on defense can run onto the court. The assistant coach determines the exact number before the ball is tossed.

Unlike the 3-on-2 drill, this drill ends if the defense gets the ball and the offense must regroup before going again. When the offense scores, the center immediately gets the ball and

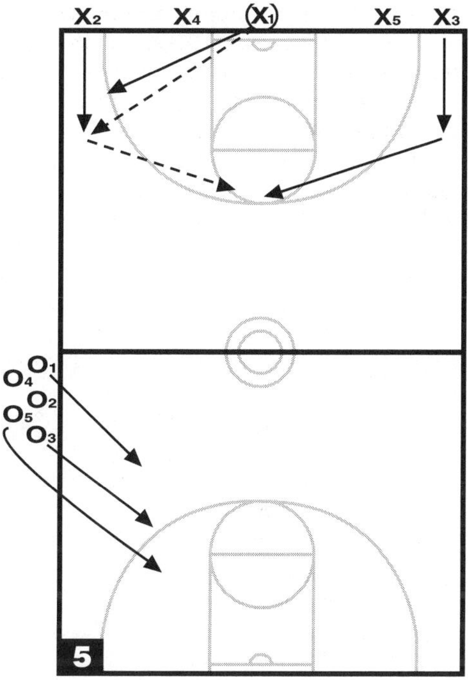

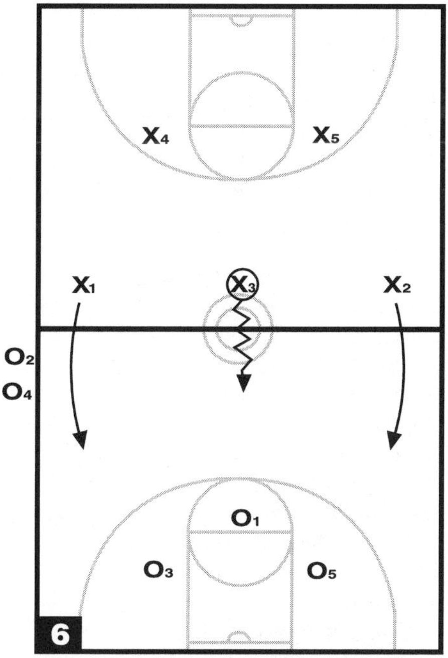

inbounds it to trigger the fast break weave in the opposite direction. The defenders on the court sprint to the other end and play defense until they prevent the offense from scoring. They may not leave and this continues until the defense gains possession of the basketball.

Once defensive possession is gained, the defenders run off the court and a new number is chosen. After five minutes, the teams switch roles and continue. The team with the most points at the end is the winner. The losing team usually serves a penalty, which can include running one suicide and one sprint following practice.

This is a great time to keep statistics. It will help the guards realize good passes from bad ones and cut down turnovers in games by one-third.

—Dennis Seman,
Northampton High School,
Eastville, Va.

All-Around Complete Game

THIS BASKETBALL formation is an excellent drill to implement throughout your practice sessions to work on both offensive and defensive fundamentals in a half court situation. With the use of three additional players, the transition from offense to defense and vice-versa is available.

The drill works best with nine players but is not limited to this number. If you have 12 participants, there would be two groups waiting to come in and the drill rotation stays the same. If you had 10 players, one team would play with three and substitute on their own to allow each player to have an opportunity to compete.

Players enjoy this drill because it works on all phases of team basketball within a structured setting. Similarly, coaches understand how the drill emphasizes the importance of communicating with your teammates, which is often times overlooked as a priority.

With the conditioning required and the competition involved, players get competitive during the drill. Motivating factors, such as the winning team being exempt from running or something similar, can be successfully integrated also.

Games are played to a predetermined amount of points or a time limit of 7 to 10 minutes. Two teams start on court with the third team on baseline waiting for a score.

If the offense scores, they must backcourt the ball behind the 3-point arc and the ball is immediately live with no waiting for the defense (new team Y) to come on the floor. If the defense gains possession and scores, they stay on offense and the team on the sidelines comes in on defense. The sideline team only comes in when there is a score. The team that gets scored on must leave the court quickly and be ready to come in on the next score.

The defensive team cannot steal the ball as it's being backcourted behind the arc after a score. They can, however, steal it after the rebound.

KEYS:

- Defensive communication, talking about match-ups.
- Quick passing, not allowing defense opportunity to get set.
- Proper offensive movement.

3's are worth 2 points, everything else counts for one point. Fouls are "checked" in at top.

—Mike Mondello,
University of Florida,
Gainesville, Fla.

SHOOTER FALLS BACK FOR DEFENSE

PRACTICE DRILLS should simulate game conditions as much as possible since you play the way you practice. The drills should reflect the concept to be emphasized within your system.

This drill incorporates many facets of the game of basketball, such as developing a full-court mentality, creating outnumbering situations, working on rebounds and outlets, sprinting to fill in the lanes, conditioning players and, above all, improving on transition from offense to defense and vice-versa.

The drill begins with a three-man straight or three-man weave. The player taking the shot must fall back for defense while the other two players work on rebounding and outletting the ball to initiate the fast break. It becomes 2-on-1 throughout. This drill must be run for 2 minutes.

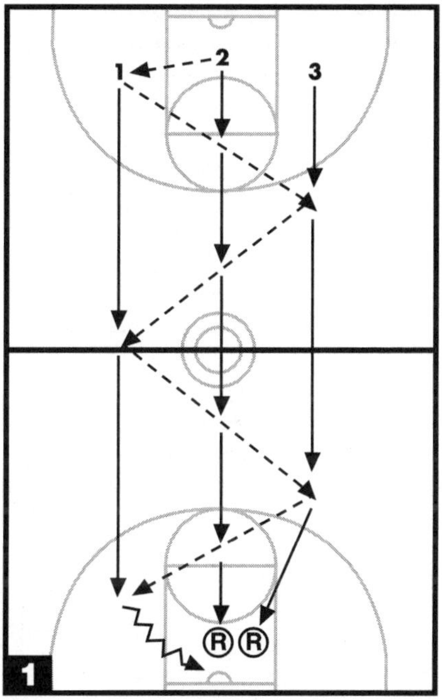

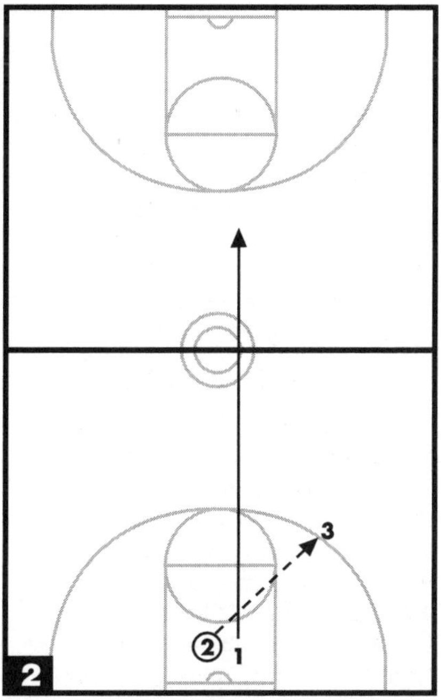

6 POINTS TO EMPHASIZE

1. The shooter falling back for defense must sprint to a position between the man and the basket and keep the player in their vision.

2. Teammates must communicate.

3. Players must be quick in giving an outlet pass or inbounding the ball to initiate a fast break to maintain the game-like intensity.

4. Players should avoid dribbling and make more passes.

5. After taking a shot, the player sprints straight in the paint—don't let them make a "banana cut."

6. Shooter falls back for defense.

—Vinod Vachani,
Head Girls; Coach,
Welham Girl's High School,
Dehra Dun, India

"Lady 'Stangs"

THROUGHOUT PRACTICES, I've always tried to come up with new and innovative ways to stimulate game situations, especially drills which involve thinking skills and basic basketball skills. We forget about the mental aspect of basketball and expect players to master this without prior practice.

Last season I developed a new drill we call "Lady 'Stangs" since our mascot is the Mustangs. It has since been one of my most productive drills and I use it nearly every day in practice. The girls really get up for this drill and always give 100 percent the entire time it's run.

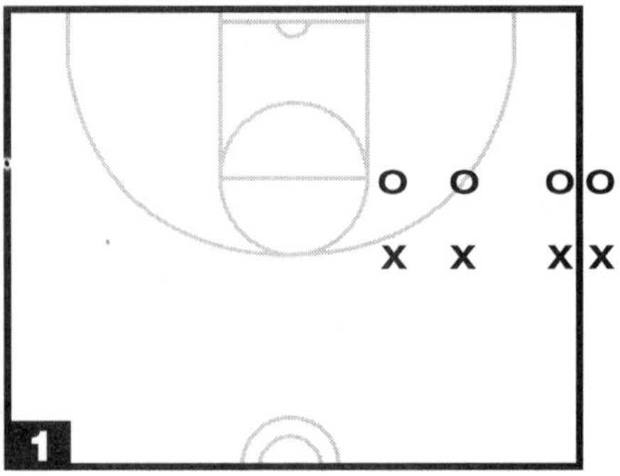

Divide your team into two evenly—separated groups according to ability. One team plays offense for 5 minutes (or whatever amount of time you find appropriate) while the other team plays defense for 5 minutes. The roles are reversed during the next 5 minutes.

2-ON-2 PLAY

The teams play 2-on-2 until a basket, defensive rebound or turnover occurs. The catch is, as seen in the diagram, that once the two offensive players have finished, they must pass the ball to the coach and run to half court. Once the coach passes to one of the two players behind the line, they pass to the one of the two new offen-

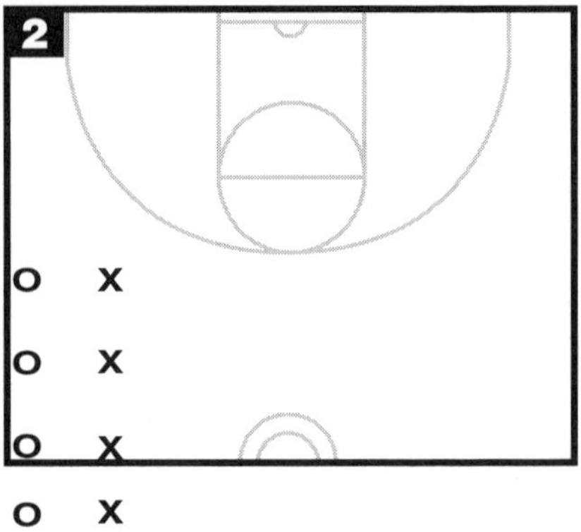

sive players who are defended by two new defensive players. After the pass, the two passers return to the offensive line. This continues for 5 minutes.

We keep track of the score and time on the scoreboard during the 10-minute drill so players know how far they are ahead or behind. Scoring can be accomplished by both the offensive and defensive teams.

The offensive team can score points by draining a basket (1 point for a 2-point shot and 2 points for a 3-point shot) and getting an offensive rebound (2 points).

The offensive team may also call one time out per 5 minutes if they cannot get the ball in to their player. This results in only a 1 point penalty instead of the normal 3-point penalty.

The defensive team can score points by causing a turnover (2 points) or denying the initial pass for 5 seconds (3 points). We tell our players that the initial pass must be made inside the 3-point line or it's considered a turnover. This makes it tougher to get open, as opposed to running out to the passer.

PASSING IS PERTINENT

We emphasize that good passes from out of bounds are just as important as the

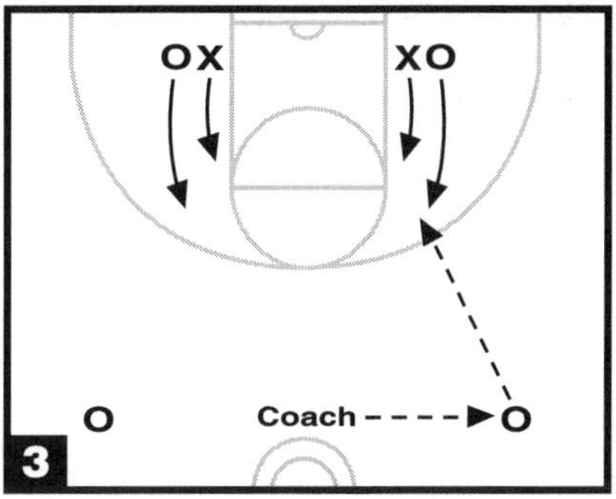

players working to get open. Plus, stopping an in-bounds pass for 5 seconds should be recognized as a real accomplishment. We instruct our players to use picks and screens to keep the defense honest, as well as encourage teamwork between the two offensive players.

This drill enhances any practice and covers all aspects of a game situation: defense, offense, passing, boxing out, screens/picks and taking the ball out of bounds.

We've been pleased with the results of this drill and feel it's just one reason why our team has been so successful.

—Ray Kues,
Head Girls' Coach,
Bishop Brossart High School, Alexandria, Ky.

4-On-4 Touch the Line

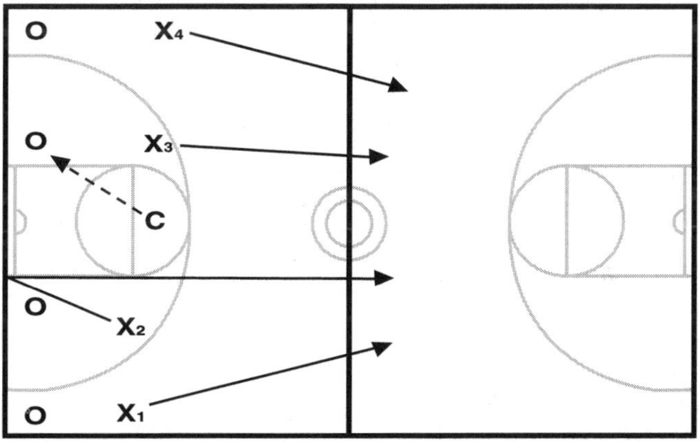

THE DEFENSE IS facing the basket, while offense has its back to the basket. The coach calls out the name of one defensive player (X2). That player must touch the baseline while X1, X3 and X4 retreat to defense.

A coach throws the ball to any offensive player and the offense attempts to execute a fast break. The defense must talk and work together to cover the open man. X2 must recover quickly to pick up the open man. Have your offense run a motion game.

On a basket, the defense takes the ball out of bounds and becomes the offensive team. The offensive team becomes the defense and must play full-court, man-to-man denial defense. Play continues until a basket is scored.

Emphasis with this drill is on talking, helping and reacting.

—Mack McCarthy,
Virginia Commonwealth,
Richmond, Va.

Five-Ball Drill For Success

THIS DRILL features full-court passing, shooting, running and team confidence. I learned it a few years ago from a junior coach running it. It's a wonderful drill I have used ever since.

RULES:

1. Set the game clock to 5 minutes.

2. On one side of the clock, set the number of points (100) the team wants to score as its goal during the drill. Be realistic about the number of points that can be scored by your team.

3. You need at least nine players and five balls. With too many players, enough repetition is not possible and conditioning is limited.

4. On each trip, 3 points can be scored on two outside shots and one layup.

5. Subtract 1 point for each missed layup.

6. The key to the drill is how fast the middle player can run the court.

7. Dribbling is allowed only to avoid traveling.

DRILL 1: The middle player starts by passing the ball and running to the left. The other two players at the first stations begin running the floor as the ball is passed between the three players moving down the court. The ball is returned to the middle player for a layup at the opposite end of the floor.

The two players on the wing bounce off the baseline for a cross-court pass from the wing players at the opposite end of the floor, who are waiting to run the drill.

The jump shot should be taken from at least 12 feet. The jump shooters rebound the ball, pass to the wings and rotate into the lines under the basket. The middle player under the basket then begins to run the drill in the opposite direction as the players who just passed the balls go for the jump shots.

Set realistic goals for your players. If the goal is not achieved in 5 minutes, run the drill again. The point of the drill is to establish team accomplishment.

NOTE: Wings can cross under the basket instead of bouncing off the baseline and receive a pass from the near player. Do not let players take a second layup. A missed layup costs a team 1 point.

—Dennie Bridges,
Head Men's Coach,
Illinois-Wesleyan University,
Bloomington, Ill.

"In basketball, personal goals have little meaning. Team goals are the only ones that really matter."
—Jack Ramsey

2-Man Break

THIS DRILL IS DONE simultaneously on both sides of the floor.

SHOOTING LINE

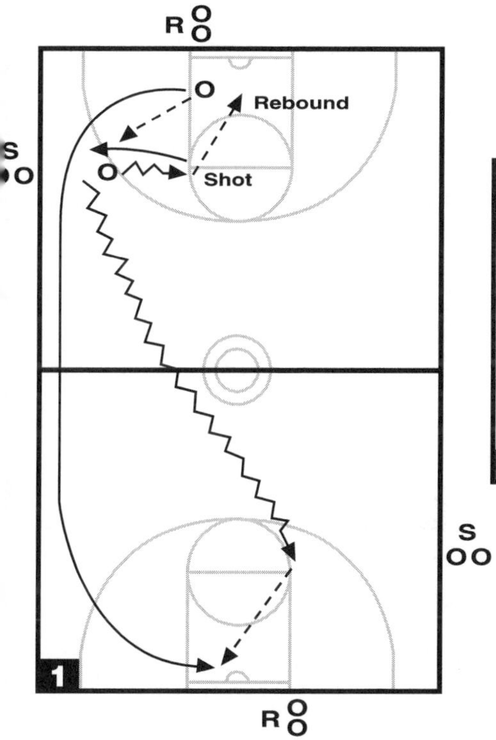

1. The player dribbles to the elbow and shoots a jumper, then gets to the free-throw line extended for the outlet pass.

2. Outlet—show the outside hand and turn outside once the player receives the ball.

3. The player must dribble full court to the opposite elbow and pass to R for layup.

4. When the ball returns to the free-throw line, the player passes for a layup and v-cuts to the opposite elbow for a jump shot.

REBOUNDING LINE

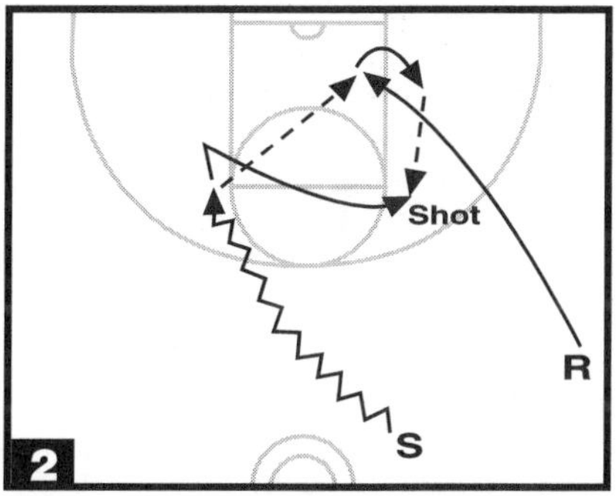

1. The player rebounds the shot and then outlets to S.

2. The player sprints down the floor through the hash mark for a layup.

3. When the ball goes back to the free-throw line, the player must jump stop, pivot outside and pass back to elbow for jumper.

—Patrick Dugan,
Head Coach,
Homer Central High School,
Homer, N.Y.

"One thing that I don't believe in is excuses."
— Karl Malone

AN EFFECTIVE TRANSITION DRILL

ALL COACHES ARE looking for drills that are game-like in nature. The following has all the different transition situations a team is going to face in a game (1-on-0, 2-on-1, 3-on-2, 4-on-3 and 5-on-4).

As the diagram shows (W = white jersey and G = green jersey) the drill begins with one player with a ball under the basket and two players on the opposite team beside them.

The player with the ball begins dribbling to the other end. As they reach the foul line, the other two players chase them. This is the 1-on-0 portion of the drill.

After a shot is taken, the two defenders will attack the other player down the floor. This is the 2-on-1 portion of the drill.

After a shot is taken, the first offensive player rebounds or takes the ball out-of-bounds and outlets to one player who attacks the two defensive players to make the 3-on-2 portion of the drill.

After a rebound or made basket, the four offensive players attack the three defensive players (4-on-3).

After a rebound or made shot, it becomes a 5-on-4 situation.

Once the 5-on-4 portion of the drill is over, have your players move to different spots on the floor and run the drill again. Run this drill for a specified amount of time (typically 15 minutes) each day.

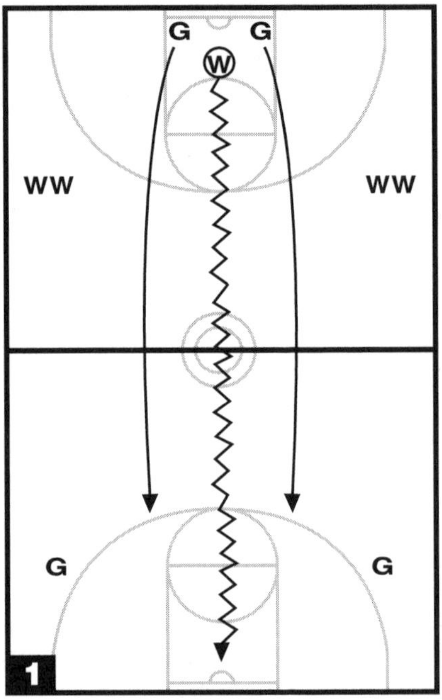

Players love this drill because they get to run up and down the floor, while coaches love it because it works in game situations.

—Bruce Thomas,
Head Coach,
Ottawa Hills High School,
Toledo, Ohio

"There's nothing like respect on a basketball team, toward the coach and toward one another."
—Lenny Wilkens

Chapter 6

CONDITIONING & STRETCHING

STRESS CONDITIONING IN THE OFF-SEASON

DURING THE PAST decade, basketball has undergone an evolution of sorts. Players have become larger, stronger and quicker.

At the root of these characteristics are weight training and conditioning programs. Instituting a solid, well-developed program is imperative if you want to build a successful basketball program. Failure to do so is accepting mediocrity.

As coaches, it's essential to make your athletes understand that weight training and hard work during the off-season directly affects your success during the regular season. We stress to our players that during the season we improve as a team, not individually. During the off-season is when we improve our individual games.

The overall goal of the off-season strength and conditioning program is to produce physical gains relative to success on the basketball court. The program needs to be structured so your athletes are challenged, but not so demanding that they give up on parts of the workout.

A maximum of 1 hour per day dedicated strictly to strength and conditioning isn't too much to ask. Getting through the first 2 to 3 weeks is the key factor, but once athletes begin to see and feel the tremendous gains this program produces it'll be hard to keep them away.

The program is structured so weight training is done 4 days per week with conditioning twice per week, along with 1 day off. It looks like this:

Monday and Thursday

Workout I (chest, shoulders and triceps).

Tuesday and Friday

Workout II (legs, back and biceps).

Wednesday and Saturday

Workout III (conditioning).

Sundays

Let your players take the day off.

WEIGHT PROGRAM

The weight program is the most vital aspect of conditioning for your basketball players in the off-season. To neglect the weights is to accept the fact that a player is just going to get behind other players who dedicate themselves.

The schedule is set so that Monday and Tuesday are "heavy days" (more weight and less repetitions) while Thursday and Friday are "light days" (less weight, more repetitions). On heavy days we work with 5 to 8 repetitions. This is where we get our greatest strength gains.

On light days we work to get 9 to 12 repetitions with each set. This is where we achieve muscular endurance and is done because basketball players need to utilize both muscular strength and endurance when they play.

Each workout should take no longer than an hour. If it does, players are resting too long between sets. Two minutes between each set should be sufficient before the muscles are ready to be worked again.

These sets should be performed in "pyramid" style. The first set of each body part (not the first set of each exercise, as those muscles are already warm) should be a warm-up set of approximately 15 repetitions. This should be pyramided by increasing the weight and decreasing the repetitions until the player's last set is the heaviest. If the athlete gets below their target repetitions, the weight needs to be decreased to get back to the desired range.

All exercises shall be done for 3 sets, except bench presses and squats, which should be done in sets of 4 since they're the biggest mass-building exercises.

Athletes should monitor on paper all work done to ensure proper evaluation and see the gains and goals accomplished.

WORKOUT #1

(Monday and Thursday)

Chest (Do 1 and 2, then maybe do 3 or 4)

1. Bench press (bar)—4 sets.

2. Incline bench press (bar or dumbbell).

3. Dumbbell flies (flat or low incline bench).

4. Dumbbell pullovers.*

Shoulders (Do 1 or 2, and 3)

1. Behind-the-neck-press (bar).*

2. Dumbbell press.*

3. Side lateral extensions.*

Triceps (Choose 2)

1. Close-grip bench presses.

2. Lying tricep extensions ("skull crushers").

3. Cable pushdowns.

4. Dips.

WORKOUT #2

(Tuesday and Friday)

Legs (Do all 4)

1. Squats (4 sets).*

2. Leg extensions.

3. Leg curls.

4. Calf raises (3 sets of 30 reps).

Back (Choose 2—pick 1 or 2, then do 3 or 4)

1. Lateral pull-downs.

2. Pull-ups.

3. Seated cable row.

4. Bent-over, one-arm dumbbell row.*

Biceps (Choose 2)

1. Barbell curls.*

2. Standing alternate dumbbell curls.*

3. Steep incline seated dumbbell curls (simultaneous).*

4. Concentration dumbbell curls.

A weight belt should be worn snugly during these exercises.

EXPLANATION OF WEIGHT PROGRAM

Maintaining proper form during all lifts is critical as bad form can cause injury and other undesirable effects. This includes using proper breathing techniques, going through the full range of motion during each rep and not cheating by using momentum or other non-targeted body parts.

The use of a spotter is very important, so players can always go for that important last rep.

1. BENCH PRESS

Bring the bar down and let it touch the chest, then drive it upwards so the bar ends up over the eyes in a slight arching movement. Keep the chest up, do not arch the back, keep the elbows directly under the bar and don't bounce the bar off the chest. Grip slightly more than a shoulder width apart.

2. INCLINE BENCH PRESS

Bring the bar down so it touches the upper chest (just below the collar bone) and press it up. If using dumbbells, stretch at the bottom and "squeeze" at the top of the movement.

3. DUMBBELL FLIES

Use a "hugging" motion, not a pressing movement.

4. DUMBBELL PULLOVERS

This is a good chest exercise if done correctly. Squat down and arch the back over a bench with the head back. Hold the dumbbell with both hands over the face and lower the weight behind the head.

Breathe deep during the lowering phase and exhale on the pullover. Have players keep the arms bent slightly and pull with the chest and not the triceps.

5. BEHIND-THE-NECK-PRESS

Go all the way down, then up. Grip should be slightly more than shoulder width.

6. DUMBBELL PRESS

Use full range of motion, simultaneously lifting with both arms.

7. SIDE LATERAL EXTENSIONS

These can be done either seated or standing. Keep elbows bent at a 90-degree angle and bring the weights up until the upper arms are parallel to the floor.

8. CLOSE-GRIP BENCH PRESS

This is the same as bench press #1 except the player's hands should be approximately 6 to 8 inches apart with the elbows tight to the body.

9. LYING TRICEP EXTENSIONS

Use an EZ curl bar. Keep the elbows pointing straight up to the ceiling and lower the bar so it touches the hairline, then extend back up.

10. CABLE PUSHDOWNS

Keep hands 6 to 8 inches apart, lower to full extension and raise only to the chest.

11. SQUATS

Feet should be shoulder width apart. Lower until knees are at a 90-degree angle and press up through the heels. Keep the back straight during the whole movement.

12. LATERAL PULL DOWNS

Use a wide grip and concentrate on pulling with the back's lateral muscles as opposed to the arms. Think of the bar as merely an extension of the bar to the laterals.

13. PULL-UPS

Have your players use an overhand, wide grip with this exercise.

14. SEATED CABLE ROW

Stretch at the bottom of the movement. When bringing the weight in, stick out the chest and "squeeze" at the top.

15. BENT-OVER ONE-ARM DUMBBELL ROW

Bend over with an arm extended and a knee over a bench.

16. BICEP EXERCISES

Go through full range of movement, "squeezing" at the top.

WORKOUT #3 CONDITIONING PROGRAM

(Wednesday and Saturday)

The conditioning program should take no longer than 35 minutes per workout and is geared toward improving quickness, agility, muscular power (explosiveness) and cardiovascular fitness.

It's vital for your players to sufficiently warmup before starting the workout. Some 5 minutes of light jogging followed by 2 minutes of light stretching should do the job. All conditioning should be done with 100 percent intensity.

Begin the workout with 4 minutes

of rope jumping. Have your players jump on both feet for 1 minute, then with only the right foot for another minute, followed by left, then on both feet again for a total of 4 minutes.

After a 1-minute rest, have your players move on to backboard touches (or wall jumps). They should jump up and hit the backboard with both hands. As soon as the feet hit the floor, explode back up without pausing at the bottom. Always keep the hands above the shoulders. Repeat for 1 minute with a 2-minute rest afterwards.

Up next are plyometrics using either 2 stairs or a 1 1/2 foot high bench. The first exercise is continuously hopping with both feet for 1 minute.

Rest 1 minute before going on 1 foot at a time. Step up with the right, up with the left, down with the right and down with the left. Go for 1 minute.

Following another 1-minute rest, do the same but lead with the left foot this time. Again, have your players rest 1 minute before hopping with both feet for another minute. Rest 2 minutes upon completion of plyometrics.

DO THE FOLLOWING QUICK FEET EXERCISES

We now go to the quick feet drill. This drill improves agility and is especially good for big men.

A. Up And Back

1. Have your players start at one end with their feet straddled at positions A and B.

2. Jump to position C with both feet.

3. Jump and straddle with feet in positions D and E.

4. Without turning, repeat the process backwards and repeat for a cycle of seven up-and-backs.

B. Right Foot

1. Start on B and jump to C on the right foot.

2. Go to foot positions D, E, C, A, B in order and repeat 7 times.

C. Left Foot

1. Follow the same pattern as for right foot 7 times around.

D. Both Feet

1. Follow the same pattern as for 1 foot in a ski-like fashion. Have your players do this exercise 7 times.

Following the quick feet drill, conditioning should last for 25 minutes if the correct pace indicated throughout the workout was kept. Now cool players down with a 2 to 3 minute walk. Don't let them stop and sit down!

Stretch for the last 8 to 10 minutes. Stretching is done lightly before the workout for warm-up and is good afterwards, while their muscles are warm, to increase flexibility, reduce soreness and aid in recovery.

DEMANDING PROGRAM

This off-season strength and conditioning program is very demanding. However, each weight workout takes no longer than 1 hour and each conditioning workout takes no longer than 35 minutes.

The effects produced should not be underestimated. Remember...if it was easy, everyone would do it!

If your athletes follow this program faithfully they'll become bigger, stronger, quicker and all-around better players. Once athletes begin to see and feel the results this program will produce, you should no longer have to worry about whether they're doing their workout.

All it takes is a little time on your part to implement this program and it will produce success in the upcoming season.

–Ben Drake,
Assistant Men's Coach,
Spencerport High School,
Spencerport, N.Y.

Circuit Drill Conditioning

CONDITIONING CIRCUIT DRILLS are the most important part of any basketball program. They're among the quickest ways to work on conditioning and to get a lot done in very little time.

In the circuit drill, the fundamental work is done at game speed. Doing so not only prepares players for repeating the movement correctly in a game, but also conditions them.

Run this drill for 30 seconds and demand that everyone go all-out in order to set goals for each station. Have each player work for 30 seconds and then have their partner work for the next 30 seconds.

The partner who is not working is responsible for keeping the other player's score. Players must start and stop this drill on the coach's whistle.

STATION 1: JUMP ROPE

The player uses any normal or heavy rope and jumps for either 30 seconds or 1 minute. Their elbows must be touching the side of their body to create more wrist movement while jumping over the rope.

STATION 2: SPRINT & BACK-PEDAL

The player sprints from the end line to a hash mark set at a 30-foot line and then back-pedals to the end line, with their partner counting the number of trips made in 30 seconds or 1 minute.

STATION 3: FINGER PUSH-UP

The player gets down on their fingers and starts to do the finger push-up. On each push-up, the player must have full flexion and full extension at the elbow joint. Their partner counts the number of push-ups done in 30 seconds or 1 minute.

STATION 4: BACKBOARD TOUCH

The player stands under the backboard and jumps to touch both hands on the backboard, comes down and continues to jump and touch the backboard. Their partner counts the number of touches in 30 seconds or 1 minute.

STATION 5: DEFENSIVE STEP AND SLIDE

The player stands at the foul line and starts to step and slide from one elbow to the other. Ask your players to tuck their hands behind their back and place their fists on the knees with the back straight and the head up. Their feet should not cross or touch. The partner counts the number of trips across the key in 30 seconds or 1 minute.

STATION 6: BENCH JUMPING (OVER AND BACK)

The player stands on one side of a 2-foot bench and starts to jump over the bench and back. Their partner counts the number of jumps made in 30 seconds or 1 minute.

–Vinod Vachani,
Welham Girls' High School,
Dehra Dun, India

Increasing Performance Through Stretching Drills

HAVING YOUR PLAYERS stretch before participating in physical activity is the most important thing they can do to warm up correctly. It's also one of the most neglected areas in athletic training.

Players will work on developing their skills or on getting in better physical condition, yet seldom take time to warm up properly before participating in these activities. That's because most coaches and athletes haven't been taught or simply don't realize the extensive benefits that come from a good stretching program.

BOOST PERFORMANCE

Perhaps the greatest benefit of supplementing physical training with a regular stretching program is to improve athletic performance.

Stretching helps to loosen and lengthen your player's muscles, ligaments, joints and tendons, further assisting in increasing their range of motion and flexibility. If a player's body is limited in its range of motion and flexibility, he or she will also be limited in bending, reaching, jumping and striding to their full potential.

The natural tendency of body muscles not being used or exercised is to tighten up. Stretching helps counter and reverse muscle contraction. Muscles need to be stretched to their maximum length slowly. When done so, they perform at full potential and also more efficiently by using less energy from your body.

Research has confirmed that athletes possessing great physical flexibility most often are the better performers.

No one starts a car in cold weather and immediately drives off without letting the engine "warm up" properly. If you do, you can cause serious damage and the car will not run well or efficiently. Your player's bodies are no different. That's why before every practice, game or workout your players should completely stretch their bodies.

AVOID INJURIES

Another advantage of having your players do daily stretching exercises is to help protect against possible injuries. Reports from many trainers and coaches have produced five general conclusions when their athletes had been on regular stretching programs:

1. There was a reduced number of injuries that occurred when compared to athletes who had not been on a regular stretching program.

2. When injuries did occur, they were usually less severe.

3. Athletes recovered faster if they had been on stretching programs before an injury occurred.

4. Stretching can be extremely helpful in dealing with muscle soreness. If a player's muscles become sore, stiff or ache, have them do stretching exercises for the specific area of the body that's involved.

If they regularly experience soreness or stiffness after working out, you may want to stretch them each day immediately after practice.

5. A final benefit of a regular stretching routine is that it takes very little physical exertion. This will leave players with more energy and strength for practice and games. Stretching properly can help them perform better and prevent injuries and muscle soreness.

Remember the adage, "An ounce of prevention beats a pound of cure."

Have players spend a few minutes each day before working out to help improve, enhance and further develop their athletic performance.

RULES FOR STRETCHING EXERCISES

1. WHEN TO STRETCH

Have your players do stretching exercises before working out, practicing or playing. For extra flexibility, they can also stretch in the morning when they wake up and before they go to bed in the evening.

However, it will normally be adequate if they stretch daily only before exercising.

2. WEAR A SWEAT SUIT

If possible, have your players wear a sweat suit when they stretch to help their muscles stay warm and loosen up easier. Sweats allow body heat to be retained and aid in the stretching process.

3. MOVE SLOWLY

To begin and end any stretching drill, have your players move in and out of the stretching position slowly. Don't let them make jerky or bouncy movements when they stretch.

If a stretching drill involves continual movement, have them move slowly and gradually as they increase their range of motion.

4. HOW FAR TO STRETCH

When doing stretching exercises, have your players reach arms, legs or bodies into the stretching position until the stretch can be felt. Do not let them stretch to or past the point of pain.

5. STRETCH FOR TIME

Athletes should perform each stretching exercise for at least 15 seconds to receive the full benefit. After a week or two, have them do it for 30 seconds.

If desired, stretching time can later be increased to 45 and then to 60 seconds for each exercise. The longer they hold each stretching exercise, the more their flexibility and range of motion will increase.

A 30-second stretch for each exercise is adequate for a basketball player's stretching program.

6. DO NOT COMPETE

Do not let your players compete against others in how far they can stretch during stretching exercises. Some people are naturally more flexible than others. Have your players stretch to improve their own flexibility and range of motion only.

7. STRETCH BOTH SIDES OF YOUR BODY EQUALLY

8. STRETCH DAILY

–John W. Scott,
Assistant Men's Coach,
Salt Lake Community College,
Salt Lake City, Utah

"The harder you prepare, the luckier you get."
— Michael Jordan

IMPROVING VERTICAL JUMP

IMPROVING THE VERTICAL leap should be a goal of most basketball players during the off-season. This is the time of year when athletes aren't playing a lot of games and have more time to devote to strength training.

CREATE POWER

There are a couple of key components that must be addressed. The first component is creating more power.

A player's vertical jump is in direct proportion to the power output of their lower body. It can be defined as:

POWER=
FORCE x DISTANCE/TIME

With this in mind, the more force created over a fixed distance in a minimal amount of time translates into a greater output of power. The objective of any training protocol is to increase the force generated over a fixed distance (such as one step to the basket) and decrease the time it takes to complete that movement.

SPEED KILLS!

Speed is another component. Improving your player's speed will make them more explosive. When it comes to doing speed work, lots of coaches talk about working hard. From where I sit, it's not about working hard, but it's about working smart.

Anybody can work hard, but if your players are practicing using poor technique—no matter how hard they work—they won't get better. Practicing good form, allowing the body to rest and generally using your head will go a long way towards improving their technique.

If your basketball program doesn't have a conditioning coach, there's a great book entitled *Sports Speed* by George Dintiman. This book is full of great drills which, when incorporated with a good strength protocol, will add inches to your player's vertical leap.

On another note, jogging will not help develop a player's vertical jump. When they think running, it should be of the sprinting variety.

STRENGTH

The last component is strength. A stronger athlete is a better athlete. Once again, our main concern is being efficient. It's our objective to create athletes who not only leap high, but leap often.

Athletes must be able to fight for loose balls above the rim. There's a lot of good information on strength training but the key is to find information that you can trust and stick with it. Positive results will happen, but only in due time.

When it comes to increasing your player's "vertical," your protocol demands their total commitment. Most players just like to shoot, but by putting the ball down and enhancing their power you'll see big improvements in their game.

–Graig White,
Director of Performance Enhancement,
Rutgers University,
Camden, N.J.

GLOSSARY OF TERMS

(Note: Positional descriptions can vary based on player abilities.)

BALL HANDLER—The player who dribbles and runs the offense.

BALL SIDE—The side of the court where the ball is located.

BASELINE—The line at either end of the court that runs parallel to the backboard. Can describe players' motion toward the baseline in offensive movement.

BLOCK—The portion of the free-throw lane nearest the baseline.

CENTER—Usually the tallest player on a team.

CUTTER—Player who moves off a screen toward the basket or to receive a pass.

FAST BREAK—An offensive strategy in which a team advances the ball quickly up the court to score an easy basket.

FIELD GOAL—A successful 2-point shot.

FORWARD—A player who is usually tall and can shoot from the perimeter and rebound.

FREE THROW—A 15-foot shot taken from the foul line.

FREE-THROW LINE—A line 15 feet from the basket behind which players take free throws.

FREE-THROW LINE EXTENDED—A parallel position extended to the right or left of the free-throw line by a few feet.

HELP SIDE—Opposite the ball.

HIGH POST—The area around and near the free-throw line.

INBOUNDS PASS—Throwing the ball in play from out of bounds.

HOOK SHOT—Offensive set shot during which the player turns his or her body sideways and arcs a ball in the air toward the basket. Usually done by a forward or center.

JUMP SHOT—An attempt from the floor to make a basket, usually from more than 5 feet away from the basket.

LAYUP—A shot from very close range, usually as a player dribbles directly at the basket.

LOW POST—Area along the free-throw line.

MAN-TO-MAN—Each player is assigned the responsibility of playing against one specific player from the other team.

OUT OF BOUNDS—Outside the playing area. The area from which a pass can be made to bring the ball into the area of play.

PERIMETER—Outside the free-throw lane.

PIVOT FOOT—Offensive player must keep this foot in contact with the floor at all times when not dribbling.

POINT GUARD—Primary ball handler in the offense.

POST—Area along the free-throw lane and halfway up the lane toward the free-throw line.

PRESS—When the defense extends pressure to the half-court line (half-court press), to the free-throw line (three-quarters press) or to the baseline (full-court press).

SCREEN—An offensive player intentionally blocks the path of a defensive player.

SCREENER—An offensive player who blocks the path of a teammate's defensive player.

STRONG SIDE—Side of the court where the ball is located.

THREE-POINT LINE—Semicircle that runs around the perimeter of the basket and from beyond which a basket is worth 3 points.

THREE-POINT SHOT—Shot from beyond the three-point line.

TOP OF THE KEY—Area slightly beyond the top of the free-throw lane.

WEAK SIDE—Area of the court opposite the ball.

WING—Area to the side of the offensive setup, usually the free-throw line toward the sideline.

ZONE—When players are assigned a certain area to play instead of a certain player to play.